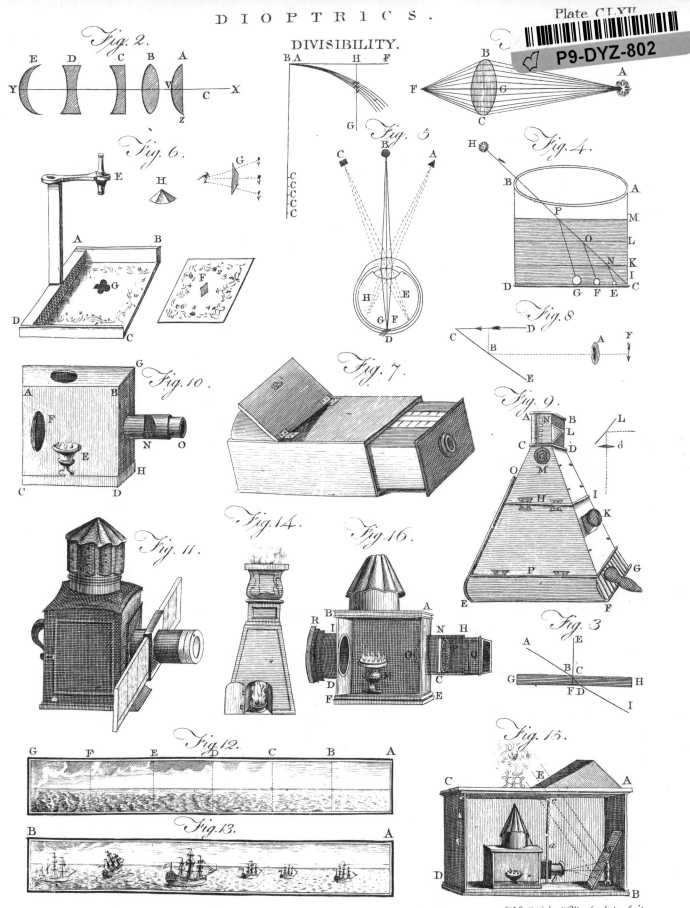

1. 'Dioptrics' from the Encyclopedia Britannica 1794.

COLLECTING OLD CAMERAS

To
my dear wife Sadie,
and our children Jeffrey, Elaine and Philip,
for their help
with both the collection and this book,
and especially to Elaine
who excels in the dual role
of daughter and secretary.

Cyril Permutt
1975.

COLLECTING OLD CAMERAS

CYRIL PERMUTT

DA CAPO PRESS · NEW YORK · 1976

Library of Congress Cataloging in Publication Data

Permutt, Cyril.
  Collecting old cameras.

  Includes indexes.
  1. Cameras—Collectors and collectors and collecting
I. Title.
TR6.5.P47 1976   771.3'1'075   76-14888
ISBN 0–306–70855–8
ISBN 0–306–80050–0 pbk.

COLLECTING OLD CAMERAS by Cyril Permutt
first published in Great Britain in 1976 by
Angus & Robertson (U.K.) Ltd.

First American Edition, 1976, by Da Capo Press, Inc.

Copyright © Cyril Permutt 1976

Published by Da Capo Press, Inc.
A Subsidiary of Plenum Publishing Corporation
227 West 17th Street, New York, N.Y. 10011

CONTENTS

1646 Portable camera obscura and the magic lantern both described by Athanasius Kircher in his *Ars Magna Lucis et Umbrae.*

1726 First images produced by light on nitrate of silver made by Johann Heinrich Schulze.

1800 Photographic images and photograms made by Thomas Wedgwood on paper and leather coated with a solution of silver nitrate, but these were not fixed; the pale images continued to darken when exposed to light, finally disappearing.

1802 Solar microscope images recorded by Sir Humphrey Davy but were also not fixed. 'An Account of a Method of Copying Paintings by Light upon Nitrate of Silver' invented by T. Wedgwood Esq. with observations by H. Davy, published in the *Journal of the Royal Institution*, June 1802.

1807 Camera lucida invented by William H. Wollaston.

1819 Thiosulphate's (hyposulphite's) power of dissolving silver chloride discovered by John Frederick William Herschel.

1827 First known photograph, taken on a pewter plate coated with bitumen by Joseph Nicéphore Niépce.

1829 Persistence of vision (basis of the cinematograph) described by Joseph Antoine Ferdinand Plateau.

1833 Phenakistoscope invented by J.A.F. Plateau.

1833 Stroboscope (wheel of life) invented by Simon Stampfer.

1834 'Photogenic drawings' on paper sensitized with silver chloride first made by William Henry Fox Talbot.

1835 The latent image discovered by Louis Jaques Mandé Daguerre.

1835 First paper negative by W.H. Fox Talbot.

1837 First successful daguerreotype taken by L.J.M. Daguerre.

1838 Stereoscope invented by Charles Wheatstone.

1839 Daguerreotype process, photographs on polished silver plates, made public by L.J.M. Daguerre.

1839 Paper negative and positive process published by W.H. Fox Talbot.

1839 Direct positive images on paper produced by Hippolyte Bayard.

1839 Sliding box whole-plate daguerreotype cameras made by Alphonse Giroux with Daguerre's seal and signature.

1839 Large daguerreotype cameras marketed by N.M.P. Lerebours.

HISTORY

1839 Miniature 8 × 11 mm daguerreotype camera made by Carl August Von Steinheil.

1840 Wooden folding camera built by Charles Chevalier.

1840 Actinometer made by Jean Baptiste François Soleil.

1840 Daguerreotype camera using mirror instead of lens invented by Alexander S. Wolcott. (This was the subject of the first American photographic patent).

1841 Calotype process (paper negatives and positives) patented by W.H. Fox Talbot.

1841 Voigtländer all-metal daguerreotype camera with new fast achromatic lens to calculations of Joseph M. Petzval (1840).

1844 First history of photography *Researches on Light* by Robert Hunt published in London, March 1844.

1844 *Obituary to Catherine Mary Walter*, the first book illustrated with a real photograph, published March 1844.

1844 *Pencil of Nature* by W.H. Fox Talbot. (In six parts, first part published 29th June 1844.)

1847 Albumen on glass negatives intro-duced by Claude Felix Abel Niépce de St. Victor.

1847 Albumen paper for positive prints pro-duced by Louis Désiré Blanquart-Evrard.

1848 Hyalotypes, first photographic posi-tives on glass, patented by William and Frederick Langenheim.

1849 Refracting (lenticular) stereoscope using lenses instead of mirrors intro-duced by Sir David Brewster.

1850 Magazine-type camera invented by Marcus Sparling.

1851 Wet collodion negative process in-vented by Frederick Scott Archer.

1851 Improved lenticular Brewster type stereoscope made by L.J. Duboscq and demonstrated at the Great Exhibition triggers off first era of great popularity for stereoscopic photography.

1852 Ambrotype (collodion negatives bleached and viewed on dark back-ground giving a positive image) de-veloped by Frederick Scott Archer and Peter W. Fry. Although published freely by Scott Archer, this process was patented in America by an American, James Cutting. The name 'ambrotype' was suggested by his friend Marcus A. Root, a daguerreo-typist.

1852 Twin lens camera (top lens was a viewfinder) made by André Adolphe Eugene Disderi.

1852 Ferrotypes (tintypes), direct positive images on japanned metal introduced by Adolphe Alexandre Martin.

1853 Microphotographs on microscope slides exhibited by John Benjamin Dancer.

1853 First twin lens stereoscopic camera made by J.B. Dancer.

1855 Folding bellows used on camera by Alphonse Davanne.

1856 Aerial photographs taken from a balloon by 'Nadar' (Gaspard F. Tournachon).

1857 Stanhopes (microscopic photographs viewed under thick plano-convex lenses) made by Sir David Brewster.

1858 Anaglyphic projection of stereograms invented by d'Almeida.

1858 Pistolgraph miniature camera made by Thomas Skaife.

1859 Magnesium light (produced by burning magnesium wire and ribbon) recommended by Professor Robert Wilhelm Bunsen and Sir Henry Roscoe.

1859 Cartes-de-visite popularized by A.A. Disderi (they were first introduced c.1852 and patented by Disderi in 1854).

1860 First *British Journal Photographic Almanack*, a one sheet wall calendar for 1860. (Given as a free supplement to the *British Journal of Photography*, 18th December 1859.)

1861 Focal plane shutter with variable slit invented by William England.

1861 Reflex camera patented by Thomas Sutton.

1864 Motion picture camera and projector patented by Louis Ducos du Hauron but not produced.

1864 Woodburytype process introduced by Walter B. Woodbury.

1871 Gelatine dry plate described by Dr Richard Leach Maddox.

1877 Series of cameras used by Eadweard J. Muybridge for first successful action pictures of galloping horse.

1877 Praxinoscope invented by Émile Reynaud.

1879 George Eastman's first patent (taken out in England for an emulsion-coating machine for the mass production of photographic dry plates).

1879 Zoogyroscope (zoopraxiscope) for projecting picture sequences invented by Eadweard Muybridge.

1885 Eastman-Walker roll holder for negative papers first produced 1885.

1887 Étiene Jules Marey makes motion picture camera taking a series of pictures on rolls of paper film.

1887 Roll film patent application filed by Rev. Hannibal Goodwin (patent not finally granted until 1898).

1888 The Kodak camera first marketed. The Number One Kodak camera cost $25 complete with sufficient Eastman American film for 100 pictures. After the photographs had been exposed, the camera was returned to the factory, where the film was developed and printed, and the camera reloaded for $10.

1888 Camera and projector with sixteen lenses for motion pictures patented by Louis Aimé Augustin Le Prince.

1889 Motion picture camera designed to use celluloid film patented by William Friese-Greene.

1891 Kinetograph camera and Kinetoscope viewer patents applied for by Thomas Alva Edison.

1893 Kromskop stereo tri-colour viewer designed by Frederick Eugene Ives.

1894 Mutoscope invented by Herman Casler.

1894 Slow motion camera (700 frames per second) built by Étienne Jules Marey.

1895 *Cinematographe (kinetoscope de projection)* patented by Louis Jean Lumière and his brother August Marie Louis Nicolas Lumière.

1895 X-ray discovered by Wilhelm Conrad Roentgen.

1899 One-shot tri-colour camera patented by F.E. Ives.

1903 Compound shutter manufacture begun by Christian Bruns and Frederick Wilhelm Deckel.

1912 Compur shutter invented by F. Deckel.

1913 Homeos 35 mm stereo camera by Jules Richard was the first commercially produced 35 mm still camera.

1913 Leica prototypes first made by Oskar Barnack.

1916 Hicro colour cameras introduced by F.E. Ives.

1924 Ermanox camera with $f2$ Ernostar lens marketed by Heinrich Erneman.

1924 First Leica production models on sale.

1927 Flashbulb using foil in vacuum, invented by Paul Vierkoetter.

1929 Flashbulb containing aluminium wire in oxygen invented by J. Ostermeier.

INTRODUCTION

CAMERAS have always fascinated me, and I have managed to keep almost every one that I have had since I was a schoolboy. It was however, not until the 1950s when I started to specialize in stereoscopic photography, that I really began my collection of early cameras.

My collection has grown to more than 150 stereo cameras, many hundreds of cameras of other kinds and hundreds of pieces of early photographic equipment. To complement and add to the enjoyment of these are many hundreds of photographic books, catalogues, ephemera and images, dating from the pre-history of photography to modern times.

Collectors will find that the history of photography divides up neatly into several sections. The camera obscuras used before 1839 change almost imperceptibly into the cameras used for the daguerreotype, calotype, and wet collodion processes, and although Dr R.L. Maddox first published the details of his successful dry plates in 1871, it was not until the early 1880s that the much higher speeds and easy availability of dry plates led to the production of new types of cameras. It was in the 1880s too, that George Eastman introduced the Kodak roll film camera, and it is a red-letter day indeed when the collector finds one of these. The releasing of the photographer from the necessity of producing his own sensitive material led to a great upsurge in the popularity of photography, and it is from the 1880s onwards that collectable cameras really begin to multiply. From that time until the 1920s, great and increasing numbers of both plate and roll film cameras were produced, and the collector's difficulty will be that of selecting and specializing, rather than where to find them.

During the 1920s a new breed of cameras began to emerge, using a smaller format and larger aperture lenses. 35 mm and small roll film cameras soon dominated this field, and collectors clubs such as the Leica Historical Society in Great Britain and similar organizations in other countries have come into being to cater for those of us who have specialized collections of these types.

Quality 35 mm rangefinder cameras led the way with $2\frac{1}{4}'' \times 2\frac{1}{4}''$ twin lens reflex second, and 35 mm single lens reflex trailing behind; whilst large numbers of folding and box type roll film cameras were bought by the snap-taking public. Cameras from this period too, are plentifully available for the collector who will soon learn—but alas be unable to convince his suppliers—that most of the cheaper box and folding cameras are uninteresting and practically worthless.

Collectors are able to watch both the decline and disappearance of the roll film folding cameras in the 1950s (although they are now reappearing briefly in the Chinese Peoples Republic), and also the ousting from public favour of the 35 mm rangefinder cameras by the 35 mm single lens reflex, which is only now being challenged by top flight 6×6 cm and 6×7 cm single lens reflex cameras of modern design, and we can still find good reasonably priced examples of folding and rangefinder cameras for our collections.

Extra small and extra large format, press-type, stereoscopic, panoramic, aerial, and underwater cameras can be collected either historically, or as specialized sections of the collection, and the finding of an unusual or outstanding one brings zest and joy to any collector.

The growing interest now being shown in the history of photography, and the rapidly growing number of camera collectors has created need for a book which will both encourage new collectors, and assist those already concerned with collecting early cameras and photographs.

This book is neither a catalogue nor a history of photography, although a background is needed by collectors and is included here, but is written by an enthusiastic student of the subject in the hope that together we may preserve the history of one of mankind's great discoveries.

The subject matter itself has shaped the book. The who, what, why, when and where of collecting come first in chapter one, and the other chapters are an outline of some of the items that can be collected. The advent of commercially available dry plates and roll film in the early 1880s makes a happy and obvious watershed between chapters two and three. The success of the cinema added to the impetus given to lens and emulsion technology by World War I determines the dividing line between chapters three and four; and each of chapters five, six and seven could well be an entire book in itself.

Recent discussions initiated by the *British Journal of Photography* (editorial 18th May 1973) have suggested that it is now no longer considered correct or necessary to use the initial capital when writing about the daguerreotype process, and I have similarly omitted it for the calotype and other early processes. Although we are now using metric measurements in Great Britain, I have retained the Imperial inch where it was originally used, as I feel that this helps to bring out a little of the flavour of the period. Throughout the book, I have used the exchange rate of $4 to £1 sterling until 1940, and approximately $2.50 to the £1 after that.

I would like to thank the many individuals and organizations who have helped me with encouragement, and especially those who have donated items to my collection. To mention Mr B.E.C. Howarth-Loomes, Mr Brian Coe, Curator of the Kodak Museum, the Royal Photographic Society, the Leica Historical Society, the Stereoscopic Society, and the Third Dimension Society, amongst many others in Great Britain; the Photographic Historical Society of New York, and the National Aeronautical and Space Administration, in the United States of America, is to name but a few of the many good friends and groups of friends that I have made whilst collecting early cameras.

The Rev. Dr. Cook, calotype by David Octavius Hill and Robert Adamson, 1843.

COLLECTING

THE prices of old cameras and their accessories have gradually risen as collecting them becomes more and more popular all over the world. Public auctions of early cameras, photographs, and accessories, have accelerated this trend. If the prices reached at sales such as that of the Albert E. Marshall collection of old photographic prints and books at the Swann Auction Galleries in New York on 14th February 1952, or the auction of early photographs, cameras and accessories held at Geneva on 13th June 1961, are compared with those reached in the sales at the Parke-Bernet Galleries in New York on 7th February, 20th and 21st November 1970, the increase in the level of prices becomes painfully obvious.

A striking example is seen by comparing the group of 200 original photographs made by various early processes during the 1840s, which sold for $75 (£30) in 1952, with the $2,400 (£960) paid for a group of 129 unmounted daguerreotypes in 1970.

Great interest was created among the general public as well as in camera collecting circles when the President and Council of the Royal Academy decided to sell their now famous Hill and Adamson albums at Sotheby's on the 13th December 1972. The Hill and Adamson partnership came into being in 1843, when David Octavius Hill the artist, witnessed the establishment of the Free Church of Scotland. Sir David Brewster who as a minister was involved in this matter, showed Hill a calotype portrait and convinced him that photography would be the only possible way to obtain the almost five hundred portraits needed for the giant picture of all those present that Hill proposed painting, before they dispersed to their homes.

The three albums presented to the Royal Academy contained 258 calotypes chosen from the estimated 1,500 that the partnership of Hill the artist and Robert Adamson the photographer made in some four and a half years. Withdrawn from Sotheby's sale in response to public protest, the albums were sold to the National Portrait Gallery in January 1973 for the then unheard of sum of £32,178.50 which was donated by an anonymous benefactor, and this price was reflected in Sotheby's sale on the 24th May 1973, when individual Hill and Adamson prints brought prices ranging up to £700 each. Another illustration of these rising prices can be seen in Fox Talbot's calotypes of *The Chess Players*. Two slightly different poses of these two gentlemen playing chess have been sold at

The Chess Players. This calotype by W. H. Fox Talbot 1843 was sold at Sotheby's in 1973 for £720

Sotheby's, the first on 21st December 1971 brought £430, whilst the second on 24th May 1973, brought £720.

How did I start collecting cameras? Asking a collector that is like asking him how he breathes—it just comes naturally! I found that I began to stand and look into camera-shop windows, instead of just passing by. Antique stalls drew me like a magnet, and I began to read carefully the small print of advertisements in photographic magazines, and to search diligently through the classified advertisements in newspapers and periodicals.

The favourite advertising magazine of many British collectors is of course the *Exchange and Mart** weekly. In its very first issue, published on 13th May 1868, one of the advertisements read:

Photographic apparatus—complete set for portraits $5'' \times 4''$, and views $7'' \times 6''$, also stereoscopic lens etc. Total cost about £18. Wanted in exchange a garden roller engine and barrow, but open to offer.

* [Today, after more than a hundred years, it still carries pages of advertisements of cameras and apparatus—both old and new—and many interesting items can be found in its books, magazines and general collecting pages. The *Antique Trader* is the equivalent US magazine, which also lists many Flea Markets, where early cameras and photographs are often found.]

Quarter plate 'Royal Mail' postage stamp camera 1908. One of these was found by Mr. William Lane of St. Johns, Newfoundland, some years ago, and another with three lenses was in Christies' sale on July 25th 1974.

One way of estimating the prices to pay for the type of old camera that might be found in these places is to beg or borrow a copy of the *Monark Price Guide for Photographic Retailers*. This strictly trade publication, which is distributed monthly by arrangement with the Photographic Dealers Association to subscribers only lists most of the still and cine cameras and accessories made since the 1920s that are readily available, showing their recommended list prices, second-hand prices, and trade-in values.

With the entire history of photography to choose from, the only limits to a collection are those imposed by money, time and space, and collectors will find it easy to select a theme around which to compile a collection.

At the first meeting of photographic collectors and historians in England held at the Kodak Museum at Harrow, on 28th March 1969, the areas of interest recorded included:

1. Development of modern cameras 1925–1940.
2. Early cinematograph films.
3. Early prints and images.
4. Exakta cameras.
5. History of photography.
6. Instruction books.
7. Kodak cameras.
8. Leica cameras.
9. Magic lanterns.
10. Motion picture apparatus.
11. Old accessories (lenses, shutters, etc.).
12. Pre-1900 books and catalogues.
13. Pre-1920 cameras, still and cine.
14. Pre-cinema and early cinema items.
15. Pre-war *British Journal Photographic Almanacs*.
16. Reflex cameras.
17. Stereoscopes and stereograms.
18. Stereoscopic cameras and equipment.
19. Still cameras 1880–1940.
20. X-ray photography.
21. Zeiss cameras.

and there were of course many overlapping fields of interest.

In addition to these, the Photographic Historical Society of New York lists the following collecting themes amongst its members:

1. American Civil War photographs.
2. Biographies of famous photographers.
3. Box cameras.
4. Daguerreotypes.
5. Dark room equipment.
6. Early American cameras.
7. Early aviation photographs.
8. Early examples of all makes of cameras.
9. Early roll film cameras.
10. Early wood and brass cameras.
11. Eastman cameras.
12. Glass plate negatives.
13. Historic prints.
14. Lantern slides.
15. Leica copies.
16. Panoramic cameras.
17. Photographs of early photographers.
18. Rolleiflex and Rolleicord cameras.
19. Signed original photographs.
20. Sub-miniature cameras.
21. Technical photographic books.
22. Wet plate cameras.

Collectable cameras and their associated items are still available but because of natural wastage and the rapidly increasing number of collectors, fewer items are now appearing on the open market, and much early apparatus is thoughtlessly destroyed when it should be in a museum or collection. This has led to a considerable increase in the prices of early cameras and their accessories with a consequent increase in the value of collections.

Horne & Thornthwaite wet plate triple lens stereoscopic camera 1865.

Large numbers of interesting roll film cameras can still be bought quite cheaply, however, and the enthusiastic collector will find many inexpensive ambrotypes, tintypes and stereographs with little difficulty. At the other end of the scale, $2,600 (£1,040) for a daguerreotype camera, £1,500 ($3,759) for a Victorian camera with 18-carat gold fittings in place of the usual brass, and $2,000 (£800) for a ninth-plate daguerreotype portrait of Henry David Thoreau, the American author (1817–1862), are some of the prices that have been paid for outstanding items.

Camera Care

Collectors should beware of cameras in need of what dealers sometimes refer to as 'slight repairs'. The very early cameras were usually made of wood with simple movements and shutters, and it is not difficult to replace missing parts or to repolish them. Examples from about the 1890s onwards, however, tend to be a very different proposition. Whilst reblacking or replacing scuffed leather or an odd screw or two is not too difficult, shutters, especially, tended to become more and more complicated, and specialized repairs can cost more than a camera of that period is worth.

Wooden cameras, stereoscopes, and similar pieces of equipment, should be attended to before being put with your collection. They should be carefully brushed out—adhesive tape is excellent for getting dust and debris out of awkward corners—and then wiped over with a clean dry cloth, great care being taken with the lenses and

TRYING!

"*NOW*, LADIES, *IF* YOU PLEASE! LOOK STRAIGHT IN MY FACE WHILE I COUNT FIFTEEN, AND *PRAY* DO NOT LAUGH!!"

*"Trying!" by
Gerald du Maurier.
Punch cartoon 1869.*

any other glass. A rub over with a swab of cotton wool or a soft lintless duster soaked in a mixture of equal parts of oil of turpentine (or turpentine substitute) and linseed oil—constantly turning the swab or duster so that a clean surface is always being used —will work wonders with dirty wood. For very dirty or cracked wood a clean-off with a mixture of one part of oil of turpentine and two parts of linseed oil, and then a good soaking with linseed oil alone will be of great help. The linseed oil should be applied very liberally to the surface of the wood and be allowed to soak in, any excess being wiped off after twenty-four hours. This can be repeated as often as necessary (a warm temperature assists the oil to soak into the wood) until the aged, dried-up wood comes back to life.

All wooden cameras and equipment newly acquired for a collection should be carefully examined for traces of woodworm,

and if any is present it should be treated by injecting a suitable insecticide into the holes. A hypodermic syringe with a large sized needle can be used for this purpose, though some insecticides are sold in special injector bottles. Unless they are most unusual or of real historic value, the collector would be well advised to think twice about acquiring any such items. Should any be bought, they should not be put with a collection until they have been most carefully treated and quarantined, and all traces of any infestation has been dealt with.

For polished wood in good condition a wipe over with a swab just moistened with linseed oil and then a polishing with a dry duster is often quite sufficient. My wife has her own pet recipe for keeping furniture in fine condition. She uses a solution of one part vinegar in ten parts of water. A swab, just moistened, is used, followed by a brisk polishing with a dry cloth. This is excellent for cleaning well polished woodwork, and will keep it in good condition. Ordinary white soap and warm water is very good for removing dirt and grease marks from polished wood, and a little oxalic acid will bleach out most ink stains.

For all wooden items in a collection I strongly recommend an occasional polish with one of the proprietary brands of furniture polish containing a woodworm deterrent, but I must emphasize that when a liquid or polish of any kind is used, only the smallest possible amount should be applied. The treatment can be repeated as often as is necessary and, so long as very small amounts are used, little harm can be done.

Optical black paint is marketed for the inside of cameras. But a hard wearing cellulose- or plastic-based paint, or a matt black enamel, should be used for the inside of lenses and lens hoods. Gloss black enamel or car touch-up paint can be used on worn black metal parts. Leather can be refreshed with a very slight application of scuffed shoe polish well rubbed in and polished, and the special leather dyes made for shoes can be used in very bad cases. The polish sold by antique dealers for preserving the covers of leather-bound books is excellent for leather that is still in good condition.

Clean brass with a fine patina should just be gently wiped over, or at the very most cleaned with a gentle non-abrasive liquid cleaner. Should the brass be badly tarnished, however, an impregnated pad or very fine wire wool may be necessary, and these should be used in gentle strokes in one direction only. It may be found advisable to remove all the brass trimmings and have them cleaned and re-lacquered. Antique dealers can be most helpful over this, particularly if you are a good customer, and many small metal craftsmen are also prepared to undertake this kind of work.

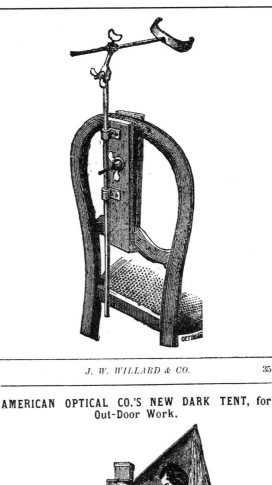

Headrests were an essential part of the Victorian portrait photographers equipment.

American Optical Co.'s new dark tent.

J. W. WILLARD & CO.   35

AMERICAN OPTICAL CO.'S NEW DARK TENT, for Out-Door Work.

For 11 x 14 Plate, ...$75 00
  Larger sizes made to order.

PHOTOGRAPHERS' TENTS,

Of all sizes, made to order, furnished with Toilet and Chemical Rooms, Ventilators, Sky-lights, and all the requisites for a Traveling Photographer.

AMERICAN OPTICAL CO.'S PATENT DRY PLATE BOX AND SHIELD, for Field Photography.

No. 1, Stereo. to hold 12 4 x 7 Prepared Plates, with Shield, ..$33 00
" 2,   "   "   18   "   "   "   .. 35 00
" 3,   "   "   12 4 x 8   "   "   .. 35 00
" 4,   "   "   18   "   "   "   .. 37 00
" 5, landsc'pe"   12 6½ x 8½   "   "   .. 45 00
" 6,   "   "   12 8 x 10   "   "   .. 55 00
  Larger sizes made only to order.

19

Quarter plate sliding box wet plate camera 1860.

Folding wet plate camera by Horne & Thornthwaite 1858.

'The Butcher Shop' from a wet plate negative 1860.

Thomas Sutton's panoramic wet plate camera made by T. Ross of London 1861 fitted with Sutton's patent spherical water lens of 1859 also made by Ross, and complete with curved focusing screen, four curved wet plate backs with unused curved glass plates, and the original curved tank for sensitizing the plates. This camera was sold at Christie's on the 24th January 1974 for the world record price of £11,025 ($25,360). Courtesy of Christies.

be rolled up like a cigarette and then torn in half, the soft torn edges being used on the lenses.

Lens cleaning fluid should be used most sparingly on old lenses. Obstinate dirt and grease can be removed with a little distilled water, methylated spirits, or cigarette lighter fluid. Carbon tetrachloride can also be used, but it gives off vapours that can be dangerous; a lens tissue slightly moistened with the liquid should be used, and the lens dried off right away with a fresh tissue. The small cotton-wool-tipped sticks that can be bought in chemist shops are very handy, as soft cotton-wool picks up dust and dirt very easily. These, and the lens tissues, should be discarded as soon as they become even slightly soiled.

A set of watchmaker's screwdrivers and a pair of small pointed nose pliers will be found helpful in making minor repairs, and the slightest smear of lubricating oil will often free seized-up metal parts. As always, apply only the slightest trace of oil, and flintless dusters should be used. A lens cleaning outfit, consisting of a blower brush, an anti-static duster, and lens tissues, should also be kept at hand.

Lenses and glass should be handled most carefully and not removed from the apparatus or taken to pieces, unless this is absolutely necessary. As much dirt and dust as possible should be blown off—aerosol containers of inert gas for this purpose are sold by photographic dealers, but a large-sized ear dropper or a small empty plastic bottle, well washed and dried, give a more gentle jet of air—and then a very soft camel-hair brush, or blower brush, should be used on them. They should then be given a final polishing with a lens tissue. This should

Collecting Pre-photographic Items

Cameras used by those pioneers of photography Niépce, Daguerre and Talbot, would seem to be the obvious starting point for a camera collection; but nevertheless, most collectors look for even earlier items than these.

The improvement in the general standard of living, and the rise of the middle class at the time of the industrial revolution in the late eighteenth and early nineteenth century, created a demand for inexpensive pictures and portraits. This has left us with a legacy of collectable images such as the silhouette and physionotrace, and items of apparatus including the camera lucida, Lorraine glass and zograscope. These were the precursors of photography and should be represented in any good collection of photographica.

Silhouettes were made extensively from the second half of the eighteenth century, and are indeed still being made today. Early silhouettes can still be easily found,

Wollaston's camera lucida 1807. Courtesy of the Royal Scottish Museum.

Zograscope 1750. An early example of this device, later models were of a more elaborate construction.

Scioptric ball, 1650. When fixed into the shutter of a darkened room to be used as a camera obscura, it could be swivelled in any direction giving a much more extensive field of view. This was the first piece of equipment specifically designed for a camera obscura and is the earliest item that can be found by a camera collector.

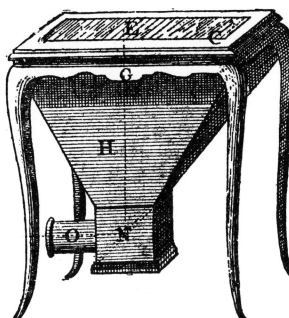

Guyot's table camera obscura 1770.
  O – lens
  N – mirror
  H – dark chamber
  E – opaque glass screen

priced about £2 to £5, depending on size, condition, and subject. As most of them are anonymous, a well known name or a date should be looked for as this will enhance the interest and value of any item in good condition.

The camera lucida, first described by William Hyde Wollaston in 1807, was a device by means of which an artist saw an apparent image of the scene or subject before him on his drawing paper. It was not a camera—a lightproof chamber—at all. The two nicest ones in my own collection were bought about a year ago, the first, bought in an antique shop was priced at £12 while the second, found a little later on a stall in a street market, cost £2, and illustrates the fact that whereas in other

fields of collecting, prices can be ascertained by referring to sales lists maintained over a period of many years, because of the relative newness of early camera collecting, prices are still very fluid.

A convex black glass mirror in a leather case, called the Lorraine glass was another of the optical devices used by artists during the eighteenth century. It gave a reduced reflection of the scene in front of the artist helping him to reproduce the correct perspective. Although not uncommon at the time, I have never seen one offered for sale. The example in my collection was given to me as a sweetener when I closed a deal for some equipment a little while ago.

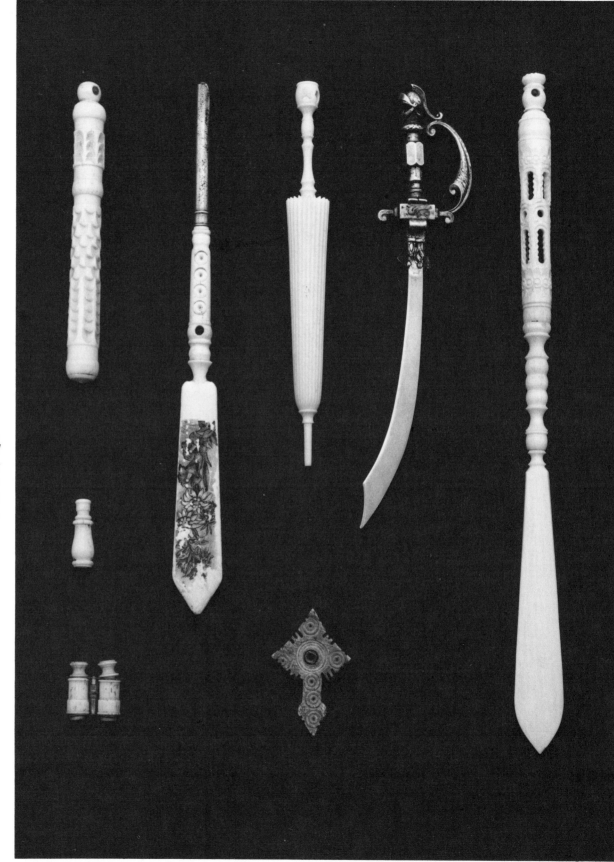

A selection of 'Stanhopes', 1860. Microphotographs and powerful tiny Stanhope magnifying lenses were combined to produce these attractive photographic novelties.

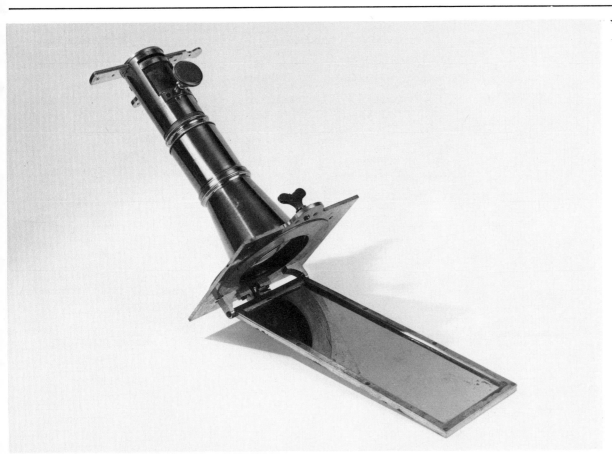

Solar Microscope, 1800. Thomas Wedgwood, (Sir) Humphry Davy, Fox Talbot, Hippolyte Bayard and many others used solar microscopes in their early photographic experiments, making this an important early instrument for the collector.

The zograscope, a movable mirror and magnifying glass on a stand, was made during the later half of the eighteenth century; it magnified and enhanced the perspective of pictures viewed with it, giving them an almost three-dimensional appearance. Sometimes called a Sheraton shaving mirror by antique dealers, collectors should be able to recognize it as an interesting item. Special perspective pictures, *vues optiques*, made to be viewed with the zograscope can also be found.

A keen collector will come across many other interesting optical curios. The scioptric ball was being used to make entire rooms into camera obscuras as early as the seventeenth century. A lens was fitted to each end of a hole drilled through a wooden ball, and the ball was fastened into an aperture in the door or window shutter of a darkened room throwing an inverted picture of the outside scene onto a suitably placed screen. Scioptric balls are now extremely rare and valuable.

During the eighteenth and nineteenth centuries peepshows of all types were popular. Miniature peepshows called Stanhopes, in which microphotographs were viewed through a Stanhope lens, were much favoured by the Victorians. The Stanhope lens had been invented by Charles Stanhope in the eighteenth century. It was a cylinder of glass with the ends shaped as a biconvex lens, and was originally used as a simple high power microscope lens. Stanhopes, often found in the handles of bone or ivory paper-knives, can still be bought for a pound or two, though I have seen one in a recent American catalogue priced at $35 (£14). They fell into disrepute as many were made holding indecent photographs. More interesting and more valuable, are the microphotographs on microscope slides first made by John Benjamin Dancer in 1853.

Collecting Camera Accessories

Lenses

Lenses are collectable in their own right. The large brass and glass lenses used on early cameras made delightful exhibits, whilst the names on them read like a photographic 'Roll of Honour'. W.H. Wollaston, whose meniscus lens, invented in 1812, was used by Niépce and Daguerre, and has been used in countless millions of cheap box cameras ever since; Voigtländer's, established in Vienna in 1756 as instrument makers, who used Professor Joseph Petzval's calculations to bring out the first photographic doublet lens, the Petzval Portrait lens, invented in 1840; and Lerebours et Secretan, famed Parisian opticians and camera makers (I have one of their lenses on a sliding box daguerreotype camera in my collection), these are some of the names a collector will come across.

Others include Carl Zeiss, who founded the Zeiss optical works in Jena on 17th November 1846, when photography was just finding its feet, and who, with Ernst Abbé the mathematician and Otto Schott the master glassmaker, created some of the famous Zeiss lenses; Andrew Ross, who made lenses for many famous British calotypists and daguerreotypists; Dallmeyer, son-in-law and pupil of Andrew Ross, who invented the symmetrical aplanat or rapid rectilinear lens in England in 1866; Hugo Adolf Steinheil, who invented the same lens almost simultaneously in Germany; and Taylor, Taylor and Hobson, some of whose lenses were used by the Eastman Kodak Company in the early 1900s. Their names are legion and all these craftsmen's handiwork would be an adornment to any camera collection.

The romantic history of Bausch and Lomb, the famous American lens manufacturers, is one of great interest to photographic collectors. John J. Bausch emigrated from Germany to the United States in 1849, and although he had been trained as an optical apprentice in Germany, he had to take up woodmaking in his new home. However an accident with a circular saw took off two fingers of his right hand, and although his friend Henry Lomb collected $28 (£7) from their workmates and friends for him, Bausch, who was newly wed, soon needed to look for work again. Bausch's brother sent him a stock of spectacle frames and lenses from Germany, and he became a travelling salesman. He was barely able to make a living and in final desperation sold a half interest in his floundering little business to his friend Henry Lomb for $62 (£15.50), Henry's entire savings. A handshake confirmed the deal—in all their years together they did not bother with a written agreement—and from that small beginning grew one of America's largest optical manufacturers whose lenses will be found on some of the most interesting and collectable American cameras.

Shutters

The collector will find many early cameras with apertures marked in the old Uniform System, the more common of these and their equivalent f stops are listed here:

3	4	6	8	10	16	32	64	128
$f\,7$	$f\,8$	$f\,10$	$f\,11$	$f\,12{\cdot}5$	$f\,16$	$f\,22$	$f\,32$	$f\,45$

European cameras have shutters marked with the letters O for time and Z for bulb in place of our more customary English initials. The basis of a number of specialized collections, shutters are also an aid in dating early cameras. It will be the front shutters—those that were fitted in front of or behind the lens, or between the lens elements—that will be most interesting to the collector.

Early daguerreotypists had no need of shutters. Dr John William Draper, a professor of chemistry at New York University, gave exposures of some thirty minutes when he made what were some of the world's first daguerreotype portraits during October and November 1839. One of the first exposure tables, published in America early in 1840, gave times up to seventy minutes for outdoor daguerreotypes made during the winter. These exposures were made by simply removing the lens cap, and replacing it after the necessary time had elapsed. The earliest real shutter that I have seen is just a square of wood that drops into a frame of beading fixed around the lens of an experimental photographic camera obscura made during the late 1830s. Improved plates and processes, and the subsequent shortened exposure times, led to the invention of the drop shutter in 1845. This was just a plate with a hole in it which, when released, slid down between a pair of guide rails. These drop shutters were usually positioned in front of the lens, and the exposure was made as the hole fell down past the lens. For longer exposures an elongated hole was used, and elastic bands and springs were soon being utilized to speed the shutters for shorter exposures. Flap shutters followed in the early 1860s. Their up and down motion, which gave the foreground more exposure than the sky, was much favoured by landscape photographers. The flap and drop shutters that came soon after also gave the maximum exposure to the foreground.

Revolving shutters, in which a plate with a hole in it swung across the lens—momentarily exposing the sensitized material (some using a pair of plates moving simultaneously), and again driven by rubber

Shutters used on roll film and dry plate cameras in the 1890's and early 1900's.

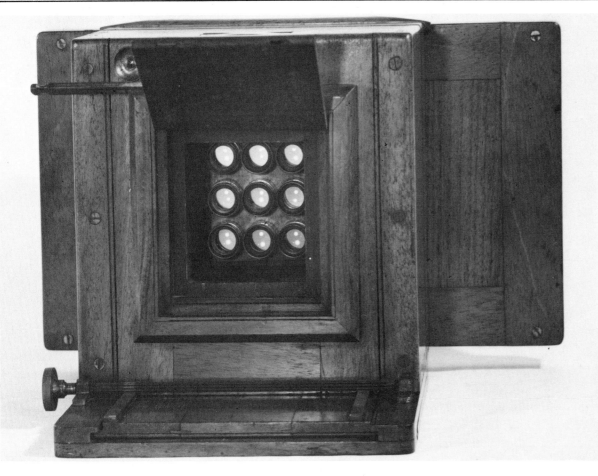

bands or springs—were another of the precursors of the modern shutter. Examples of any of these early shutters are well worth securing for a collection.

The introduction of the dry plate in the late 1870s, and then roll film in the 1880s with ever faster emulsions, soon led to the production of more accurate shutters with a wide range of speeds. An improved version of the focal plane shutter that had been invented by William England in 1861 —a blind with a variable slit that passed immediately in front of the sensitized plate or film, almost at the focal plane of the lens—was brought out by B.J. Edwards in 1880. Roller blind shutters which were similar mechanisms fitted in front of the lens, were being sold soon afterwards by Thornton Pickard, and E. and T. Underwood, amongst many others.

Air brake shutters, where the time that the blades were kept open was regulated by the movement of the piston in a small pneumatic governor, were the next step in shutter design. Typical European examples were the Compound (1902) and the Koilos (1906) both of which were made in Germany. The earlier model of the Koilos shutter (1905) used a leather brake mechanism. These early shutters are all very collectable items.

The Compound shutter made by Bruns and Deckel, who later became Compur-Werk GmbH of Munich, was followed by the Compur, the first shutter with a geared speed mechanism. Although patented in 1910, the first production models of the Compur were not on sale until 1912.

Alfred Ganuthier, who had begun manufacturing the Koilos shutter and other small camera parts in a village in the Black

Forest, soon expanded the business and by 1912 the original staff of five men had grown to some twelve thousand, producing large numbers of the Vario, Pronto, and Singlo air brake shutters, as well as many other camera parts and accessories. Their geared Ibsor shutter was introduced in 1913, and was produced until an improved Pronto with a built-in delay action device was made in 1930. Flash synchronization was introduced in the Prontor of 1938, which had five shutter blades, instead of the three that had been previously used.

When used in conjunction with pre-war catalogues, the exact dating possible with these and other shutters, will help the collector to identify many of the more obscure and unusual cameras.

Flashlight Equipment

Flash synchronization had grown out of photography's quest for artificial light sources. Although at first photography was called 'sun sculpture', methods for taking photographs when sunlight was not available were being sought from photography's earliest days. There are a few early photographs which were taken by artificial light, but very little in the way of collectable apparatus that can be pin-pointed as having been used exclusively for photography. Limelight, the intense white light produced when a rod of lime is heated in an oxyhydrogen flame, was being tried by the end of 1839, and there were experiments with many different combinations of combustible chemicals.

Fox Talbot took the earliest high speed photographs in 1851. Repeating some earlier experiments of Sir Charles Wheatstone, he used the spark from a battery of Leydon jars to illuminate moving objects, and recorded them on albumen plates. He patented the process the same year.

Magnesium was discovered by Sir Humphrey Davy in 1808, but it was not until 1864 that the blinding light it gave off was first used for photography. It is at this point that collectable apparatus first appears, as several lamps burning magnesium wire began to be marketed. One such lamp, made by Alfred Brothers, was used by Piazzi Smyth in 1865 to photograph the inside of the Great Pyramid in Egypt. Magnesium tape or ribbon was found to be better for this purpose and lamps using this were being made until well after World War I.

Powdered magnesium, available from 1866, was tried by many photographers, both on its own and mixed with a variety of chemicals. It was during the 1880s that flashlight powder (magnesium powder usually mixed with potassium chlorate) came into general use, and remained so until the advent of electric flash bulbs in the 1920s.

During this time many flashlamps were made which will delight collectors, from the complex pieces of equipment that blew a measure of magnesium powder into the flame of a spirit lamp, to simple trays on which the powder was ignited by a lighted touch paper, a percussion cap, or a spark from a flint.

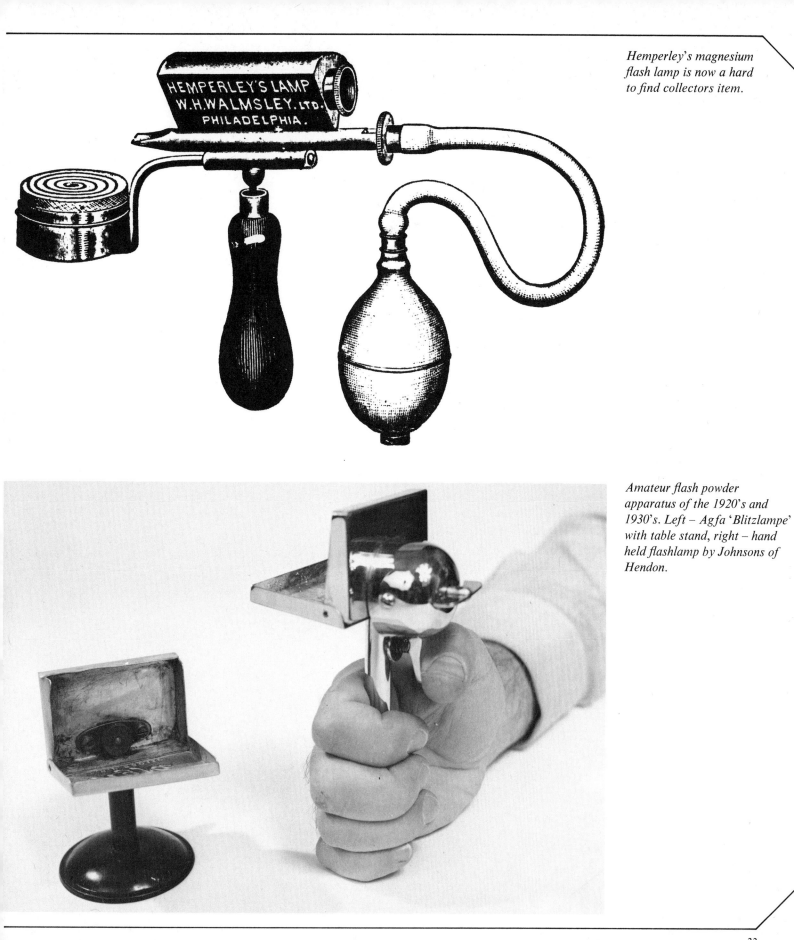

Hemperley's magnesium flash lamp is now a hard to find collectors item.

Amateur flash powder apparatus of the 1920's and 1930's. Left – Agfa 'Blitzlampe' with table stand, right – hand held flashlamp by Johnsons of Hendon.

The first flash bulbs, made in 1925, held the flashpowder in either a vacuum or an atmosphere of oxygen. They are now very hard to find. Few private collections have examples of these and they are well worth looking for. They were soon superseded by the improved flashbulb patented by J. Ostermeier in Germany in 1929. Flashpowders and the early bulbs could only be used for open flash. The lens cap was removed or the shutter opened on time or bulb, the flash fired, and the lens covered or the shutter closed. Separate synchronizers were rapidly developed, but it was the built-in synchronizer adopted by most of the leading manufacturers after World War II that led to the popularity of flash photography.

Bulbs filled with a mass of fine metallic wire, and then improved versions filled with foil shredded as finely as wire, soon followed, and the sizes shrunk rapidly to the pea-sized bulbs and the cubes that are familiar to us today. A display showing the enormous variation in the types and sizes of flash bulbs that have been made is of great interest and takes up little space.

The bright light given off when a high voltage of electricity is passed through a glass tube filled with xenon (other rare gases can also be used) is fast enough to stop most movement. At the Massachusetts Institute in 1931 Harold Edgerton developed the modern electronic flashgun that works on this principle, and early examples of these are valued by collectors.

Camera Books, Manuals and Catalogues

A multitude of photographic books, manuals and catalogues have been published since 1839, and early examples are eagerly sought by collectors.

PHOTOGRAPHIC PLEASURES

POPULARLY PORTRAYED WITH PEN & PENCIL.

BY CUTHBERT BEDE, B.A.

AUTHOR OF 'VERDANT GREEN.'

Cartoon from Photographic Pleasures *a light-hearted book on photography by Cuthbert Bede, 1855.*

We cannot all be lucky enough to find a daguerreotype manual or a copy of *Researches on Light*, the first history of photography by Robert Hunt, published in London in 1844, or even booklets such as Hunt's little *Photography Manual No. I*, also published in 1844. But items such as one of the many editions of his *Manual of Photography* published in the *Encyclopedia Metropolitana* in London during the 1850s still crop up. An 1853 copy was offered by an American dealer in the spring of 1973 for $130 (£52) and one of 1851 fetched $204 (£85) at Sotheby's in March 1975.

Many collectors have been able to put together specialized collections of books illustrated with real photographs. The first of these was a slim volume published privately as a memorial of the death of Catherine Mary Walter who died 16th January 1844. She was the eldest daughter of John Walter II who was at that time the chief proprietor of *The Times* newspaper in

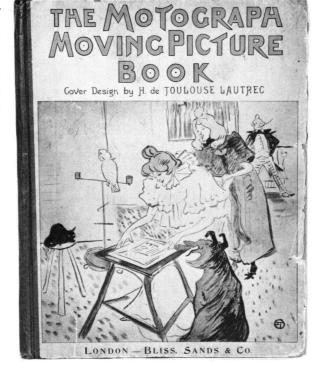

(see text)
↑
Henneman

*Calotype by ~~Hernaman~~ of a
bust of Catherine Mary Walter.
This was the first photograph
ever used as a book illustration,
January 1844. Courtesy of
Norman Hall.*

London. This tribute to her memory was written by her brother on 24th January 1844, and as was the practice, rushed into production and distributed soon afterwards. Printed by Gilbert and Rivington of St John's Square, London, a calotype print by Nicholas Henneman of a bust of Catherine Mary Walter was pasted in on the front page of each copy. The first copy to have been rediscovered in recent years is in the International Museum of Photography at George Eastman Rochester, New York, and I know of only six others. The Walter family have one themselves, Mr Norman Hall, Picture Editor of *The Times* newspaper, London (from whom much of this information comes) has another, and there is one each in the British Museum, The Reading Museum, and St Brides Library. The sixth was sold in May 1973 at the Palmeira Fine Art Auction Rooms, Hove, for £430. Although it does not have the same importance, this slender little book pre-dates William Henry Fox Talbot's famous *Pencil of Nature* by several months and is far more rare, as some twenty-four complete copies

of the latter, and many loose parts, have been located.

The *Pencil of Nature* was published in six separate paperback instalments. The first was issued on 29th June 1844, and although twelve had been planned, the sixth and final part was issued on 23rd April 1846. They contain twenty-four photographs in all: five in part one, seven in part two, and three each in parts three, four, five, and six. The complete set cost 3 guineas when published, but the last one to come to light was sold at Sotheby's sale on the 21st December 1971, for £2,500.

Very collectable items are books with wonderful titles like *The Art of Photography. Instructions in The Art of Producing Photographic Pictures in Any Colour, and on Any Material, for the Use of Beginners; And also*

'The Open Door' by Fox Talbot from his book The Pencil of Nature *originally published in six parts from 29th June to 23rd April 1846.*

Portrait of Professor McDonald from an album containing 41 calotype portraits taken between 1855 and 1860 which was bought for £1,900 by George Rinhart the well known American dealer at Sotheby's 4th December 1973.

The first British Journal Photographic Almanac *1860 was a wall sheet calendar.*

The Daguerrian Journal was the world's first photographic magazine, 1st November 1850.

of Persons who have already Attained Some Proficiency in the Art; and of Engravers on Copper, Stone, Wood, etc. By Dr. Herman Hallcut, With Practical Hints on the Locale Best Suited for Photographic Operations, and on the Proper Posture, Attitude and Dress for Portraiture. By F. Schubert, Painter. and an Appendix Containing Brief Explanations of some of the Chemical Terms Which Occasionally Occur in the Work*. No mistaking what that one was about! It was published in Berlin in May 1853, and in English by John Weele in London in 1854. Then there are classics such as *A Manual of Photographic Chemistry including the Practice of the Collodion Process* by T. Frederick Hardwich of Kings College, London, published in London by John Churchill in 1855, or Sir David Brewster's *The Stereoscope, its History, Theory and Construction*, published in London by John Murray in 1856 (the title on the spine reads simply and majestically *Brewster on the Stereoscope*), or *Treatise on Photography* by W. de Wiveleslie Abney, published in London by Longmans Green and Company, in 1878; these and hundreds of others are still available in secondhand bookshops, waiting to be found by enthusiastic collectors.

One of my favourite photographic books is the *Ilford Manual of Photography* by C.H. Bottomley. First published in London in 1890, I have a copy of the second thousand, published on 1st December 1891. It commences, 'The apparatus indispensable for ordinary photography in the field is a camera!'

Another book with a lovely flavour, is *The Art of Projection and complete Magic Lantern Manual by An Expert*. This was published in London in 1893, and the modest author was W.C. Hughes, a self-styled 'Specialist in the Art of Projection'. At the back of the book, there is a twenty-four page catalogue of the apparatus on sale at his business premises.

Many of these books include advertisements and catalogues of equipment, and collectors will find them a great help in identifying and dating early cameras. For instance, a delightful little Academy camera —an early dry plate camera that took twelve $1\frac{1}{4}'' \times 1\frac{1}{4}''$ plates—carried no name or markings of any kind when I found it on a stall in a London street market. Careful research however located an advertisement on page 251 of Marion and Company's *Practical Guide to Photography*, published in London in 1885, which not only shows an almost identical model, but also has what is practically an instruction manual for the camera.

Instruction manuals are another interesting section for collectors, and they can either be kept on their own, or, if possible, matched to the appropriate camera.

The classic reference books for camera collectors are the *British Journal Photographic Almanacs*. The magazine itself was first published on the 14th January 1854, as the *Liverpool Photographic Journal*, the monthly magazine of the Liverpool Photographic Society. In January 1860, it became the fortnightly *British Journal of Photography* but since July 1864 it has been published weekly.

The first *British Journal Photographic Almanac* was a wall calendar and almanac for the year 1860. It was printed on a single sheet of paper and was given away free with the 15th December 1859 issue of the magazine. For the next five years these free almanacs took the form of small booklets measuring $4'' \times 2\frac{1}{2}''$. The almanac for 1866 was the first to be sold separately and in book form. It measured $7'' \times 4\frac{1}{2}''$, and was published annually for almost a hundred years in this format, for much of the time in a choice of green cloth or yellow card binding. It was not until 1964 that the

Kodak transparent film for the Kodak camera, 1896. The Kodak Museum.

almanac took its present large $11\frac{1}{4}'' \times 8\frac{1}{2}''$ format. Early *British Journal Photographic Almanacs* are now very difficult to find, two —for the years 1866 and 1869—were sold at Sotheby's on 24th May 1973 for £60.

In the almanacs, as is the case with many of the early photographic publications, it is the advertisements that the camera collector will find fascinating. Some of the issues carried a thousand pages of advertisements each. Reading through them, the collector will be enthralled to watch the gradual evolution of cameras and photographic processes. They are all shown, from the early sliding box cameras, through all the many different types that were made to keep pace with improvements in first the wet and then the dry plates.

Camera Plates and Films

Early photographic plates and films are very collectable too. Amazingly, collectors will find that sensitive material half a century old or more can still produce good negatives, often with very little evidence of their age. They should be stored in a cool place one might say the cooler the better. The Commonwealth Transantarctic Expedition of 1957–8 discovered rolls of film that had belonged to members of the Scott expedition of 1910. Frozen for almost fifty years, they still produced perfect pictures.

Sizes and emulsions of early examples vary enormously, most manufacturers having had their own recipes, and many even their own special sizes. In 1914 Kodak listed seventeen different sizes of spool for roll films, and although many more have been added since then, few of them have survived. Even once popular sizes such as the Kodak 235—spools of 35 mm film with black paper leaders and trailers made for the early models of the Exakta and Contax cameras —are no longer available, and the number of the older sizes and emulsions that do remain available decreases year by year.

Even the empty boxes and leaflets of early plates and films are worth keeping, if only to fill out the records of a collection. Leaflets, business cards, advertising posters and so on relating to them take up but little space. They can be collated in scrap books or framed and hung on walls and help to add another collecting dimension to the more usual items that form the basis of most collections.

Collectors should be particularly careful with early cellulose nitrate cinema films. The highly inflammable nitrate base begins deteriorating from the moment that it is made, giving off acid fumes which gradually destroy the silver image and attack the emulsion. The breaking down of the collodion in turn releases agents which react with the cellulose nitrate, speeding up the process. The danger of fire, and the highly toxic vapours given off, make it hardly worth while keeping these early films unless one has the necessary storage facilities. Any found in good condition should be loaned or donated to one of the recognized film archives—the National Film Archives Division of the British Film Institute, 81 Dean Street, London W1V EAA, or the American Film Institute, John F. Kennedy Center, Washington DC 20566, USA, will be pleased to accept anything of value. Any not worth keeping should be destroyed but not by burning them!

Exposure Meters

Estimating the correct exposures for any particular combinations of light, subject and emulsion speed, has always been a problem for photographers, and attempts at solving it have left behind a trail of apparatus for the collector to harvest. First to be used were exposure tables, and these are still used today. A selection ranging from simple ones to complicated mechanical models should be fairly easy to put together. Actinometers, in which a sample of sensitized paper is exposed to the light, were an early starter.

The classic actinometer for the collector is the Watkin's Bee meter. Alfred Watkins produced his first meter in 1890. The Bee was his ninth design and he made twenty different models over a period of nearly forty years. The Bee was used by pointing it at the light source and checking the time that it took for the sensitized paper to darken enough to match the sample of colour provided. Fresh supplies of the sensitized paper were stored in the back of the case.

Extinction meters which compare the subject visually with a graduated grey wedge or a series of stops were made by many manufacturers, and obsolete models are easily found. Some of the most accurate exposure meters used today, the photometers use a similar method comparing parts of the subject with a known light source.

The earliest extinction meter in my collection was made by J. Decoudun of Paris in 1888. Examples from this period are very rare today, but large numbers of optical exposure meters were made in the

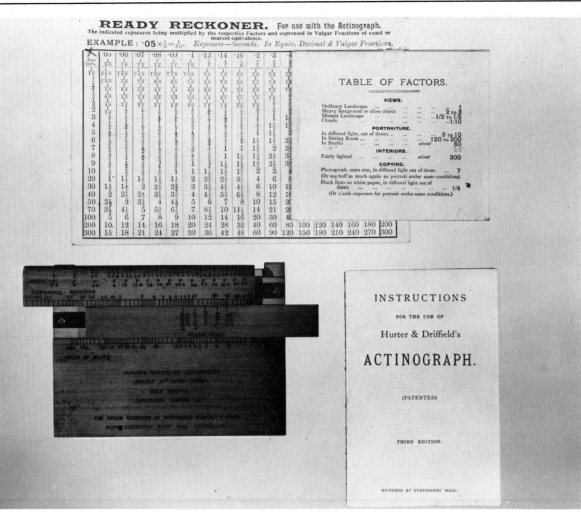

1920s and '30s and a representative collection of these would not be too difficult to put together.

More up to date, but just as interesting to the collector, are the photo-electric exposure meters in which light generates an electric current that is measured by a micro ammeter. Once again one of the *British Journal Photographic Almanacs* comes to our aid, and in the 1933 issue—printed incidentally towards the end of 1932—we find the Weston Universal Exposure Meter on page 295, and the Bell and Howell Electrophot on page 297.

The Weston Universal was model No. 617, and was advertised on page 617 in the 1933 almanac. No batteries were needed for the Weston Phototronic photo-electric cells, but this advantage was somewhat neutralized by the size and weight of the 617. Its bakelite case measured $6\frac{1}{2}'' \times 2\frac{1}{4}'' \times 1\frac{1}{4}''$, and weighed 14 oz. Light was measured in candles per square foot, and this was used with the rotating calculator dials to find the correct exposure.

Made by the Weston Electric Instrument Corporation of Newark, New Jersey, USA, the 617 was imported by Wallace Heaton Limited, who sold it in England for £20. The Weston 627 followed in May 1933. This was $2\frac{1}{4}''$ in diameter, and gave direct reading for cine cameras. The rectangular Weston model 650 was the third of this series of selenium cell meters. A number of the Weston meters in my collection were presented to me by the manufacturers to whom I am extremely grateful.

Actinometers and their accessories made by Alfred Watkins.

A selection of actinometers. The metal box (top centre) is Wynne's print meter, 1897. The French Chronoscope (bottom left) is a miniature camera that produces a negative on bromide paper without development in a few few seconds, this is compared to a set of standard tints and the exposure is read off from the accompanying tables.

The first Weston photo-electric exposure meters. Left, model 617 had two selenium cells and a sighting grove on the top, 1932. Centre, model 627, 1933. Right, model 650, 1934.

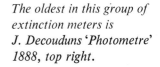

The oldest in this group of extinction meters is J. Decouduns 'Photometre' 1888, top right.

Edwardian Kodak photo-girl.

The Bell and Howell Electrophot was sold for £11 when it was first introduced. Designed for cine work, it was the same size and shape as a 100′ carton of 16 mm film, fitting neatly into the film pocket of the Bell and Howell leather camera case. Powered by a 3 volt battery, its light sensitive selenium cell indicated the aperture for a cine camera giving an exposure of 1/32 second. Known as the Rhamstine Electrophot it was produced just before the twin cell Weston 617 in the United States, but in England the Weston was the first to be marketed.

Photo-electric light meters had been made earlier than this. Weston themselves were making their model 603 early in 1932 and although they were probably used by photographers, the 603s were primarily designed for lighting engineers. It seems certain that the Weston 617 was the first self-powered photographic exposure meter on the market; but examples of any of these early models are eagerly sought by collectors.

Presentation and Celebrity Cameras

Collectors are always on the look out for unusual items for their collections and treasure cameras that have been associated with famous people. One such camera —acquired in 1944 by Dr Max Thorek, a well-known Chicago surgeon and amateur photographer of the day—had been especially made for Theodore 'Teddy' Roosevelt, and had his autograph on its bellows. General Dwight D. Eisenhower (as he was then) was also an ardent photographer. Whilst he was in Europe as the Chief of NATO in the 1950s and later, during his presidential campaign, he continually carried and used a Stereo Realist camera. This would be a wonderful item for a collection.

Probably the most expensive celebrity camera was one made at the turn of the century for the Sultan of Morocco at a cost of £1,500! This high price was not because of its technical perfection but was due to the fact that instead of brass, all the metal used in the camera was 18 carat gold. Even the screws were hand-made out of solid gold. Included in the price was a white carrying case (made of Morocco leather, of course) lined with silk velvet, and secured with gold locks and hinges.

A similar model, 'A very important 18 ct gold mounted English camera, by Adams and Co., 28 Charing Cross Road, W.C.1., the oblong body covered with red leather, the gold shutter, aperture and waist-level view finders finely chased with foliate decoration, the top with two gold wheels which operated the bellows and focal plane shutter, the back with a compartment containing five gold plate holders, the top also fitted with a chased gold-mounted leather handle, 16 inches extended, London 1901. (Said to have been presented by Queen Victoria to a European monarch.)'

was withdrawn unsold from an auction sale at Sotheby's on 1st June 1970.

It was offered to me at that time for £700. The camera was only in a fair condition, as some of the gold screws were missing, and the leather was badly worn in places. I have earlier examples of Adams and Company's cameras in my collection, and whilst they are not as ornate as this gold mounted one, one of them, the stereoscopic version of their special model 'B' of 1900, is very rare indeed.

Special presentation models of many other cameras have been made. Presentation models of the Frena made at the turn of the century, were covered with buff calf leather and had polished brass fittings.

Although I have three Frenas, one of them in mint condition complete in its original box, with the receipt, instruction manual and manufacturer's seal, I have been unable to get one of these presentation models, which are very scarce. One I missed was sold together with a Kodak No. 3 Folding Brownie Model A, at Christie's in London in December 1972, for £38, which was cheap compared with £157.50 ($362) paid for one there in January 1975.

These presentation cameras are much sought after by collectors. A lovely one was presented to Mrs Lillian Wilcox when she retired in December 1952 from Ansco's factory at Binghampton in the United States. Mrs Wilcox had joined Ansco as a young girl in 1902, soon after the E. and H.T. Anthony and Scoville and Adams companies joined together to form the Anthony and Scoville Company in 1901. She stayed on with the firm when it became the Ansco Company in 1907, and when it joined with Agfa in 1928. As a reward for her long and devoted service, Ansco presented her with 'a custom-built, gold-plated Ansco-Rediflex box-type camera' (the Rediflex was a box-built camera with a large full-

Queen Victoria presented this elegant red morocco leather camera with solid gold metal parts to a European monarch at the turn of the century.

Cartoon by Honore Daumier 1862, satirising Nadar's aerial photography.

The first American aerial photograph. From a wet plate negative of Boston taken by Professor Samuel A King and J. W. Black from a balloon 1861.

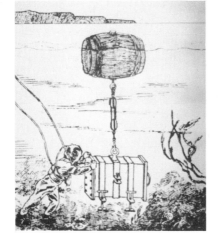

Louis Bouton using his 8″ × 10″ camera in watertight metal box suspended from an empty barrel 1894.

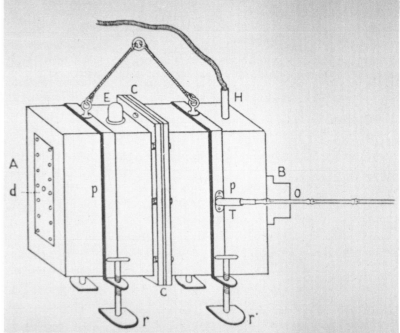

Detail of the underwater camera housing designed by Louis Bouton 1894.

size brilliant viewfinder looking, with its ƒ11 lens, like a twin-lens reflex). I wonder if Mrs Wilcox's camera is still about, or if it has found a happy home in someone's collection. Here is a fine opportunity for a collector to put in some detective work.

Many Leica cameras have had historic connections. When the American Armed Forces invaded Sicily during World War II their leader, Lieutenant-General George S. Patton, landed with a pearl-handled revolver on one hip, and a loaded Leica on the other. An M2, Leica No. 950,000 was presented to Fulvie Roiter, an outstanding Italian photographer early in 1961. Leica No. 1,000,000 is displayed in the Leitz Museum at their works in Wetzlar, and No. 1,000,001 was presented to Alfred Eisenstaedt in the summer of 1961. The millionth Leica to be produced was a major landmark for the manufacturers, but collectors are more interested in the early prototypes and first few hundred production models which change hands for hundreds of pounds today.

Eisenstaedt had been one of the earliest photo-journalists to use a 35 mm camera. Following in Dr Erich Salomon's footsteps, he at first used an Ermanox, and had indeed co-operated with Salomon on several stories. He bought his first Leica in 1930, and has used Leica cameras to take almost every photograph that he has had published since.

1961 was a happy year for anniversaries. Voigtländer, who had been making camera lenses since 1840, put their 5,000,000th lens (a Colour-Skopar X designed for their Bessamatic camera) on display in their museum in the spring of that year. This was a far cry from their celebration in 1862, which had been for their lens No. 10,000. Collectors should always be on the lookout for serial numbers of cameras or lenses that are associated with specific dates and should share this information, which is of great help in the dating of cameras in collections.

Collectors are sometimes asked inflated prices for cameras reputed to have had interesting owners, but there will be no fear of mistaking the Leicaflex that was presented to Her Majesty Queen Elizabeth II during her State visit to West Germany in 1964, for the Royal insignia E.II.R., surmounted by a crown, was engraved on the top. The gold-plated Minox that was presented to Prince Philip at the same time was similarly engraved with his initials, and should not be difficult to recognize in the unlikely event of it ever appearing on the open market. In the 1950s Her Majesty seemed to be fond of twin lens reflex cameras, and she has been photographed using several other types too. If she has kept them all, she may be a fellow collector at heart.

Specialized Cameras

Interesting collections could be formed of specialized cameras such as the fingerprint cameras made for the police, and the many varied types of cameras made for the armed forces, whilst cameras designed for aerial photography would need a book of their own.

It is more than a hundred years since Gaspard Félix Tournachon, a French photographer better known by his professional name Nadar, took the first aerial photograph. Using the Paris studio that he had opened with his brother Adrian as a base, he started by taking a portable dark room, as well as a wet plate camera up in the basket of a gas balloon.

When aerial combat began in grim earnest during World War I, the Royal Flying Corps soon found that although it was difficult enough to hit a moving target from a stationary platform, or a stationary target from a moving platform, to hit a moving target from a moving platform was a feat that required both manual dexterity and a great deal of training. The Mark III Hythe Gun camera, was designed to aid in this training. A replica of the Lewis gun in use at that time, its between-lens shutter was set by pulling back the cocking handle on the left side of the gun stock, and it was released and a photograph taken by squeezing the trigger as if firing the gun; it used 120 roll film. The pair in my collection still take excellent photographs.

Apparatus for underwater photography provides another unusual category for collecting. A camera was used underwater for the first time by William Thompson, an English engineer, at Weymouth Bay in 1856. Loaded with a dry collodion plate, the camera was sealed into a waterproof box which had a plate of glass at one end and a heavy metal tripod attached underneath. The camera lens was placed against the glass, and a large wooden drop type shutter was positioned outside. The whole contraption was lowered from a rowing boat into 18′ of water and, by pulling on a string, an exposure of 10 minutes was given.

In 1866 a Frenchman named Bazin took his camera down in a diving bell and, using electric lights powered by a Bunsen battery, took photographs in 300′ of water. Another well-known French photographer, Louis Bouton, took a series of undersea photographs in 1894, using a magazine camera in a glass-fronted watertight metal box.

Since then many weird and wonderful gadgets have been produced, and collectors can have a lovely time looking for unlikely pieces of apparatus. Specialized cameras made for most of the larger navies during both world wars have been available in surplus stores, and watertight camera housings have been made in a great variety of materials, shapes and sizes, ranging from simple wooden and plastic boxes with transparent front plates to such exotica as the Lewis Leica Photo-Machine housing that was designed by Hans Hass, and cost $300 (£120) in the United States in 1955.

The climax of such a collection might be an example of Dmitri Rebikoff's self-propelled Cine-Torpedo of the early 1950s which carried a 16 mm cine camera and a 1,000 watt xenon arc tube for lighting; or perhaps one of the amphibious cameras such as the French Calypso which cost £99 when it was distributed in London by E.T. Skinner and Company in 1962; or the celebrated Nikonos which was 'proofed against the effect of water, mud, sand, and salt sea spray'.

Many items of this kind can still be picked up quite reasonably. It is however a sad fact that when any one make of camera becomes fashionable among collectors its price inevitably rises.

Movie Cameras

Collectable items from the early forays into the search for movement on the screen include round, and long horizontal slides, each carrying a series of pictures that could be projected in quick succession. These slides, many up to eighteen or twenty inches long, were moved slowly across the lens giving a simple illusion of movement.

The mechanical slides that were introduced in the first half of the nineteenth century will intrigue collectors. The earliest of these were the slipping slides. The moving parts were painted on a separate piece of glass which slipped along horizontally behind a standard lantern slide. Often two sets of movements were painted onto the slide itself, alternate phases being blacked out by movement of the slipping glass. Later developments included the lever slides

*Toy magic lantern
cinematograph for slides
or 35mm film 1900.*

*Toy magic lantern for
rectangular or circular slides
1890.*

*Toy magic lantern for
rectangular slides 1890.*

—where moving a lever up and down imparted a rocking action to the image— and the ratchet and chromatrope slides which produced a circular motion. Dissolving views, created by the use of two, three or even four magic lanterns, and further complicated by the use of moving slides, were another step in the progress towards real moving pictures.

It was the invention of photography, and in particular the albumen process on glass publicized by Abel Niépce de Saint-Victor in 1847 and first used for lantern slides by the Langenheim Brothers in America in 1849, that really showed the way in which moving pictures were going to develop. Collectors will find that these photographic magic lantern slides make a sharp contrast to the earlier hand-painted ones.

Daguerre, famed as the inventor of photography, was, with Charles Marie Bouton, the joint inventor of the diorama. Collecting diorama pictures which measured approximately 15×25 metres is obviously impracticable; but what we can collect are the toy dioramas, the polyorama panoptiques and the toy panoramas that were made from the 1840s onward. A polyorama panoptique was snapped up by a collector in London in 1972 for £125 ($312), and the next one I saw was being offered by Vintage Cameras in their 1975 spring catalogue for £400 ($960).

All the optical toys that were so popular in the early Victorian period are wonderful collectors' items today. Peep-eggs made of alabaster with two or three scenes inside viewed through a lens in the top; peep-shows made of cardboard and linen that extended to form a perspective view; anamorphic pictures, distorted images which were viewed reflected in polished metal cylinders, or at acute angles, to restore them to normality; and kaleidoscopes, with the various kaleidoscopic tops that followed, are all interesting items.

Entertainments such as the aetherscope, which combined the scenic effects of the diorama with live actors on a stage, were a further step towards moving pictures but the problem was to be solved finally by an approach from an entirely different direction, from the phenomenon known as the 'persistence of vision'. Mentioned by Isaac Newman, Peter Mark Roget and many others, it was first put to practical use in a toy called the thaumotrope invented by Dr John Ayrton Paris in 1825. This was a cardboard disc with pieces of string attached to opposite edges, so that it could be rapidly rotated. The two sides had different but associated pictures on them, a bird on one side and its cage on the other, or a fish and a bowl, or perhaps a horse and a rider. When the strings were twisted between the fingers and thumbs the two pictures merged and were seen as one image. In the early 1830s several different devices and toys demonstrating persistence of vision were invented, and many can still be found by the collector.

In yet another of the coincidences that seem to occur so frequently in the history of

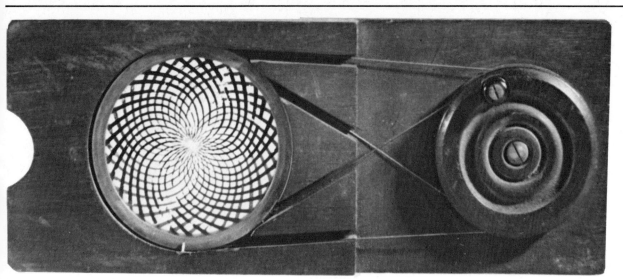

Chromatrope magic lantern slide. The two glass discs revolve in opposite directions when the pulley is turned.

Polyorama Panoptique, 1850. This is so fragile that very few are now to be found outside collections or museums.

This toy Victorian panorama demonstrates in miniature the principle of the panoramic entertainments that were so popular from the end of the eighteenth century (front and back views). Made of paper and cardboard this is another very rare item for the collector.

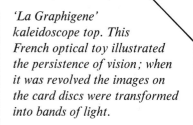

The Thaumatrope invented by
Dr. John Ayrton Paris in 1825
was a small cardboard disc
with strings attached to opposite
sides. When the strings were
twirled between the fingers and
thumbs of each hand the
pictures on the front and back
of the disc merged together.
Courtesy of the Science
Museum.

'Startling Effects' Punch cartoon by Charles Keene 1879.

The Zoetrope was invented by W. G. Horner of Bristol in 1833. It was named The Zoetrope in 1867. It consisted of a series of drawings inside a slotted drum, which, when revolved gave a semblance of moving pictures. Courtesy of The Kodak Museum.

Professor Emile Reynaud patented the Praxinoscope in Paris in 1877. Instead of viewing the pictures through slots, they were reflected by a series of mirrors. The movement of the images was much better than that shown in the Zoetrope.

54

photography the phenakistoscope was invented simultaneously in 1833 by Joseph Plateau in Belgium and by Simon Stampfer —who named his instrument the stroboscope—in Austria. The appearance of motion in the phenakistoscope was created by revolving a slotted disc in front of a mirror. The reflections of a series of consecutive images positioned between the slots, when viewed through the slots, blended together into an apparently continuous flow of motion. The images of the stroboscope were viewed through a separate slotted disc, giving the same illusion of movement.

The zoetrope, invented in 1833 by Dr W.G. Horner of Bristol, England, was a slotted vertical cylinder with a series of pictures drawn or painted on the inside. When it was revolved, the pictures seen through the slots seemed to move naturally.

I have examples of these last three devices in my collection. But the praxinoscope, invented in France in 1877 by Emile Reynaud in which the moving images were pictured in twelve mirrors arranged around the centre of the revolving drum, and the praxinoscope theatre first produced in 1879 in which the lid of the box, together with the movable scenery provided, formed a stage setting through which the mirror reflections were viewed, are much more difficult to find.

Many variations of these instruments were produced, but it was the projecting phenakistiscope invented in 1853 by an Austrian army officer Baron Franz von Uchatius which was the first projector to use a maltese cross and shutter movement to produce an even flow of motion on the screen from the intermittent pictures projected.

During the 1860s and '70s a number of people suggested using batteries of consecutively fired cameras to record a series of animated pictures for use in these early viewers and projectors. Henry Heyl of Philadelphia was in 1870 probably the first to use a series of individual photographs with his phasmatrope in which they were viewed in rapid succession.

In the 1870s when the horse was the most common form of transport, and horse racing was the most popular sport, there was much controversy about the movements of a horse's legs when trotting and galloping. A booklet in my collection *The Delineation of Animals in Rapid Motion* (a paper read before the Royal Dublin Society), published in Dublin in 1877, contains many illustrations of horses in motion drawn by the author M. Angels Hayes, R.H.A. In 1872 Eadweard Muybridge began taking his famous series of photographs in an attempt to split up the motion, and examine the actions of the horse. Many of his later series of photographs were reproduced in his monumental book *Animal Locomotion. An electrophotographic investigation of consecutive phases of animal movement* which was published in 1877. Selections of the photographs were also sold separately, and much of the book was republished in two volumes *Animals in Motion* in 1898 and *The Human Figure in Motion* in 1901. These have been reprinted many times, but the original publications and the lantern slides of the illustrations are now very rare indeed. It is these originals rather than the facsimile editions that collectors should look for. In 1880, Muybridge designed his zoopraxiscope which projected a series of photographs printed on a round glass plate. The original can be seen in the museum at Kingston upon Thames in Surrey, where he was born in 1830 and returned in 1900. together with many other interesting items that he bequeathed to the museum when he died in 1904.

The kammatograph, which first appeared in 1898, was one of the best examples of this type of projector with up to 600 pictures arranged spirally on a 12″ circular

glass plate. Not made in any considerable quantity, and rapidly becoming obsolete, they are now a wonderful addition to any collection of early cinematograph apparatus. An Olikos moving plate camera made in the 1890s, which took a similar series of pictures on an oblong plate was sold for £160 ($400) at Sotheby's on 24th May 1973.

Professor Etienne Jules Marey invented a camera for recording a series of images on one plate. Working in France in 1882 he made a rifle-shaped camera for photographing birds on the wing, and his camera of 1887 which used a roll of sensitized paper was probably the world's first successful motion picture camera. In 1888 Louis Aimé Augustin Le Prince, another of the originators of the cinema developed a combined cinematograph camera and projector which used a $2\frac{3}{8}''$ strip of gelatine film. A year later he brought out a projector with a maltese cross mechanism, and then one that was fitted with an arc lamp. In 1890 he visited his brother who lived at Dijon in France. He took the train from Dijon to Paris on 16th September and vanished, never to be seen again. Although a thorough investigation of his disappearance was made, no trace of him was ever found, and the work of one of the earliest pioneers of the motion picture was brought to an untimely end. Somewhere, perhaps in Leeds where much of his last work was done, perhaps in his bags and baggage which disappeared with him in France, perhaps even in London, Chicago or New York where he lived and experimented with moving pictures, someone may well stumble across a collectors' treasure trove of unique quality and value.

In 1889 William Friese-Greene, with the help of Mortimer Evans, built and patented a camera for photographing moving objects, but this took only 3 or 4 frames per second. The camera that Friese-Greene patented in 1893 was almost the same as the camera that had been patented by F. H. Varley in 1890. All these cameras used rolls of flexible film, and are rightly considered to be among the originators of the basic patents for the motion picture cameras that we know today.

The kinetograph camera and the kinetoscope viewer, patented by Thomas Alva Edison in 1891 and developed in his laboratories with William Dickson, used strips of celluloid film produced by John Curbutt, an Englishman who had emigrated to the United States in 1893. Although his kinetoscope was a viewer and not a projector the Edison patents established the 35 mm width and the four perforations

The Filmless Cinematography of the New Century.

"Kammatograph"

For taking and projecting Animated Photographs.

SPECIALLY CONSTRUCTED FOR THE AMATEUR.

Weight 8lbs.

Price
£6 10s.

Negative and Positive Plates 2/6 each.

Subject Plates 3/- each.

6d. allowed for every returned plate.

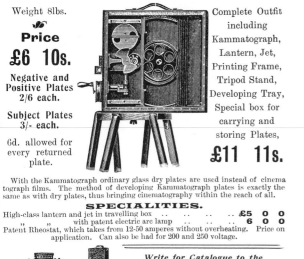

Complete Outfit including Kammatograph, Lantern, Jet, Printing Frame, Tripod Stand, Developing Tray, Special box for carrying and storing Plates,

£11 11s.

With the Kammatograph ordinary glass dry plates are used instead of cinematograph films. The method of developing Kammatograph plates is exactly the same as with dry plates, thus bringing cinematography within the reach of all.

SPECIALITIES.

High-class lantern and jet in travelling box £5 0 0
" " with patent electric arc lamp 6 0 0
Patent Rheostat, which takes from 12-50 amperes without overheating. Price on application. Can also be had for 200 and 250 voltage.

Write for Catalogue to the Manufacturers—

L. KAMM & CO.,
27d Powell Street, Goswell Road,
LONDON, E.C.

per frame that were, with slight modifications, to become the world standard for motion picture film.

August and Louis Jean Lumière used 35 mm film in the *Cinematographe* that they developed in France in 1895. At first their film had one round perforation per frame but they soon decided to join Edison in using four perforations per frame so as to make their films interchangeable. Mutoscope viewers were another approach to the problem of producing moving pictures. Using the flip book principle invented by Herman Casler in 1894, they were popular from the late 1890s until World War I. Kinora viewers were a small home movie table version of the same idea. Special cameras took 640 1″ wide pictures on 40′ rolls of negative paper strip; the subsequent positive prints came to life when flipped over in the viewer. I have several interesting kinoras in my collection including an early Lumière model. But I have turned down several mutoscopes that have been offered to me as, like many collectors, I find them too bulky and heavy for the space available.

Collectors will find cameras and projectors that use films of all shapes and sizes, for although the Lumière brothers had shown the way, it was not until 1907 that the standard 35 mm film with four perforations per frame became generally accepted. Many different film widths were used; the sprocket holes varied in shape, position, and

in number from eight perforations per frame to none at all.

Splendid collections of motion picture films can be made and this is another field that may excite the interest of the potential collector. The deeper one looks into a history of photography, the more and more evident it becomes that a camera collector must specialize and try to create a collection that illustrates fully the type of cameras and items of ancillary equipment in which he is most interested.

As the movies became more and more popular exhibitors were soon converting houses and small halls in the rush to capitalize on the new invention, and by the 1920s they were building huge Oriental-styled Moving Picture Palaces in which the public were beguiled (in a comfort that many had never experienced before) with thrills, laughter, drama and, of course, sex, all contained on reels of 35 mm celluloid.

By the early 1920s the moving picture industry was one of the five largest in the United States. Picture Palaces were built everywhere, each one larger and more luxurious than the last. There was very little room in all this for the amateur, and amateur cinematography as we know it today did not exist.

Although several manufacturers had introduced cameras and projectors, using 17·5 mm film, it was the introduction of 16 mm reversal safety film in 1923 that opened up the amateur market and brought the cinema into the home. The first 16 mm camera designed to use reversal film was the

Cine Kodak Model A. This camera, together with the Kodascope Model A 16 mm projector, were to do for moving pictures what the first Kodaks had done for still photography.

Kodak's only competition at this time, and the next item for the collector, was the 9·5 mm reversible cinematograph film and equipment that was produced by the world renowned firm of Pathé Frères. Charles Pathé had started in the cinema business in 1894 by buying one of the first Edison's kinetoscope viewers to be sold in France. The following year he obtained a cinematograph projector and films from the Lumière

The Debrie 'Sept' made in Paris in 1922 held 17 feet of 35mm film and could be used for either still or cine photography. This camera has its original black enamel finish. Courtesy of The Kodak Museum.

The 35mm cine-sept made by André Debrie of Paris. All the other examples that I have seen are finished in black enamel. This camera which was sold at Christies on 24th January, 1974 for £89 ($205) may have had the finish stripped off by a previous owner. Courtesy of Christies.

(Right) The Midas 9.5 cine camera/projector with battery container, 1933.

This Kinora viewer, 1900, with twenty reels was sold for £220 ($550) at Sotheby's salesrooms on 24th May 1973. Courtesy of Sotheby's.

(Left) Clockwork Kinora 1900. Courtesy of The Kodak Museum. One of these was sold for £200 ($500) at Sotheby's on 24th May 1973.

Silk program of what was probably the first cinema Royal Command Performance.

Wooden table model Kinora, 1900. Photograph E. A. Blyde.

The Kinora camera 1911 could take 640 frames on a 40 ft spool of one inch wide paper negative. Courtesy of The Kodak Museum.

The Model A 16 mm cine Kodak camera and the Kodascope Model A projector 1923. Courtesy of The Kodak Museum.

Brothers, and by 1896 he had taken his three brothers into his business and founded Pathé Frères.

Their 9·5 mm Baby Cine camera and projector were both much smaller and lighter than the Kodak Model A cine equipment, and were much less expensive. 9·5 mm film was supplied in easy loading daylight chargers. When processed it was returned in special cassettes and threaded almost automatically through the projector. The use of one central frame-line sprocket hole meant that the effective area of the frame was not much smaller than that of 16 mm film.

Most of the standard 35 mm cameras and projectors will be too large for the average collector to entertain, but the smaller and more portable ones are well worth looking for. The Photo-Ciné Sept, made by Debrie to a design patented by J.B. Tartara and marketed by the Société Française Sept in Paris in 1922, was one of the nicer of these smaller cinematograph cameras.

The Bol Cinegraph which was made in Switzerland, used a 76′ spool of standard perforated 35 mm cine film. This unique hand-cranked camera not only took, printed and projected cine films, but could also be used to take still pictures and to enlarge and project them. I am still looking for one of these for, although they sold well on the continent, few seem to have been imported into Britain.

Further attempts were made to produce combined camera-projectors, but without great success. Notable ones to look for are the Campro which first appeared in 1927, and the Midas which was produced six years later. The Campro was unusual because it could use either the standard 9·5 mm cine film or a special paper-based film which was illuminated from the front and projected by reflection!

The Bolsey 8 was a unique miniature still or cine straight eight camera.

An early trick picture. The taxi cab apparently cuts off the man's legs. (A legless cripple was used with prop legs.)

In 1930 the first 8 mm Homovie camera appeared, pioneered by the Kodel Electric and Manufacturing Company of Cincinnati. In this system the frames were half the width and half the height of a normal frame on 16 mm film, but the film was not split, the picture being taken and projected in the full 16 mm width; this camera is really a milestone for collectors.

It was however the Cine-Kodak Eight-

20 camera of 1932 and its companion Kodascope Eight-30 projector which introduced the then novel concept of taking 8 mm pictures first down one side of a strip of double perforated 16 mm film and then up the other. When processed the film was split down the middle, and then the two halves were joined to produce one continuous reel of 8 mm film. The great advantages offered by 8 mm film were the smaller, lighter and less expensive cameras and projectors, and of course the dramatic cut in film costs. The 25′ spools of film used were when processed the equivalent of 100′ of the standard 16 mm film.

As amateur cine-photography became more popular the market grew big enough to attract almost every large camera manufacturer, and many of the smaller ones. Collectors who are excited by the history and pre-history of the cinema will find a vast selection of cameras and equipment to choose from but, because there are so many interesting ones, the collector must be very discriminating in his choice or a collection can easily become unwieldy. A few representative cameras in excellent condition will be much better than a motley group of second-rate examples.

Amateur interest in movie making was greatly increased by the introduction of Kodachrome 16 mm cine film in 1935. The best colour film yet produced and the first really successful one for amateurs, it was invented by two musicians, Leopold Manns and Leopold Godowsky. They were taken on to the Kodak research staff in America where they further assisted in its final development and marketing.

The colour positive reversal film Kodachrome was completely free from grain, as all the silver in the emulsion was removed in the final processing. The resultant image was of such high quality that by 1941 it had been adapted for 35 mm professional use.

Called Monopack Technicolor it was used to photograph the film *King Solomon's Mines* for which Robert Surtees, A.S.C., the Director of Photography, received the 1950 Academy Award in Colour Photography.

Another cine-camera which has had many descendants was the Filmo Straight Eight made in 1935. It used 30′ loads of single run 8 mm film and was in its day the world's smallest camera. In 1936 a second model, the Filmo Double Eight, was introduced, using the standard double run 8 mm film; variants of this camera, later named the G.B.—Bell and Howell Sportster, were still being sold in the 1960s. The post-war Bolsey 8 camera was even smaller, measuring $3\frac{1}{8}'' \times 2\frac{3}{8}'' \times 1\frac{1}{8}''$, and was probably one of the most unique cameras ever made. It was designed to be used as a straight eight cine camera and also as an 8 mm sub-miniature still camera. As a cine camera it had only one speed, 16 frames per second, but when used as a still camera a variable shutter controlled by a dial at the front of the camera gave a choice of speeds from 1/50 to 1/600 seconds. This tiny instrument was a fine example of precision work and had a lovely satin chrome finish. The special 25′ magazines of single run 8 mm film which it used gave over 1,900 single exposures, or 2 minutes of screen time—or any combination of these—and the clockwork motor had only to be wound twice to expose the lot. It was indeed a little marvel and worthy of a place in any collection of cameras.

Photographs

The many different types of collectable photographs—calotypes, daguerreotypes, carte-de-visite, and so on—will be dealt with in detail in later chapters, but it is worthwhile pointing out here to collectors the wide range of material available to them.

Calotypes and daguerreotypes have always been valued by collectors as examples of the earliest practical photographic processes, but even undistinguished carte-de-visite portraits of anonymous people by unknown photographers are now in demand, and those by famous photographers, or of well-known personalities now fetch fabulous prices. A carte-de-visite full figure portrait of Isambard Kingdom Brunel photographed by Robert Howlet, was sold at Sotheby's on 14th May 1973 for £45, which is a staggering price for a photograph that was mass produced.

Leather photographs are another of the oddities much sought for by knowledgeable collectors. Thomas Wedgwood, son of the famous potter, was the first to make photographs on sensitized leather *c*.1800, but he was unable to fix the image that he made. Black and brown patent leather was used for a short while in the 1850s in processes similar to the ambrotype and tintype. Black paper was also used as a base for this type of photograph, but both leather and these black paper photographs are very rare. After searching for many years it is only recently through the sharp eyes of a good friend, that I have managed to obtain a photographic portrait on leather for my collection.

Everybody collects photographs these days—even if they are only their own snapshots—but prints of many of the greatest photographs of all time are available to collectors at very reasonable prices. Amongst others, the Imperial War Museum in London has a collection of some five million photographs. Most of them date from 1914 but they also have many dating back to the earliest days of photography. Copy prints are available to the general public at nominal prices. The even larger collection of more than six million photographs held by the British Broadcasting Company's *Radio Times*' Hulton Picture

The Hunters, from a wet plate negative 1860.

Library, does not supply prints to the public, but loans them for exhibition or publication at current commercial fees.

Smaller, but perhaps choicer collections, are the quarter of a million prints held by the National Maritime Museum at Greenwich (mainly of seaports, ships and naval items) and the forty thousand available at the Science Museum in London which include record photographs of many of the very early cameras and associated items in the photographic section of the museum. Prints of many of these can also be purchased.

There is a treasure trove too at the Victoria and Albert Museum in London's South Kensington. Their collection of photographs was started by the National Art Training Schools. These became the Royal College of Art, and in the 1850s the early photographs which had been accumulated to assist art students in their work were lodged in Marlborough House. The collection now includes some of the best work of photographers such as Fox Talbot,

Rachel and Laura Guerney by Julia Margaret Cameron, 1872. Courtesy of The Kodak Museum.

David Octavius Hill and Robert Adamson, and Roger Fenton. It even boasts a mint copy of Fox Talbot's *Pencil of Nature*. The Victoria and Albert Museum not only provides prints for sale, but also makes the originals available to bona fide inquirers for copying at the museum, and no fee is charged for this service.

Finest of all are the sepia collotype prints of some of the masterpieces in the collection of the Royal Photographic Society. The quality of these reproductions is really excellent. The Society sells these at reduced prices to members and this, together with the Society's Museum and Historical Group, makes membership a must for collectors.

The collector will be able to find great photographs wherever he lives. In America, the United States Library of Congress, Prints and Photographs Division, at Washington DC 20540, has about four million photographs on file, ranging all the way from early daguerreotypes and the works of Fenton and Brady, right up to the present day. They will supply prints of any that are not still copyright at very reasonable prices.

There are also many other important collections in America. The International Museum of Photography at George Eastman House, 900 East Avenue, Rochester, NY 14607, has more than ten thousand prints and negatives. The Art Institute of Chicago, Illinois, has some fine work of early photographers such as the portraits of Julia Margaret Cameron, and the far west photographs of Tim O'Sullivan, as well as the work of many modern masters. The California Historical Society, at 2090 Jackson Street, San Francisco, 5, has over a hundred thousand Californian photographs, and prints of these are on sale to the public too.

Only a few localities have been mentioned here, for much of the fun of collecting lies in the discovering of your own sources. Your local library or museum can be of great help in this. The British Museum in London, for instance, has several original photographs made by Roger Fenton, that may not have been seen elsewhere.

The true collector will of course try to find originals rather than copies for his collection. Although this is becoming more difficult, it is not so very long since H. Armour Smith, looking through a disused attic in Yonkers, NY, found some daguerreotypes of battlefield scenes that had been taken by an unknown photographer during the Mexican War of 1846–48. This cannot be compared with Roger Fenton's extensive coverage of the Crimean War, but it nevertheless pre-dates his work by eight or nine years, and was a most important find.

French photographic picture postcard posted from Dunkirk to Hanoi, Indo-China in 1907.

Photographic Postcards

Picture postcards have been collected since they were introduced in the days of wet plate photography. Rowland Hill originated the 'penny post' in Great Britain in 1840, but the first postcards were introduced in Austria in 1869. In Great Britain, the Post Office issued the first postcards in 1870, when the postage on them was $\frac{1}{2}$d. During that same year they were brought out in Germany and Switzerland, and they were first used in the United States and Serbia in 1873.

The earliest local view photographic postal cards were printed on 'printing out paper' by the photographer who had taken the photograph. These days, the cards are printed by large automatic machines. Early

postcards can cost as little as fifty for £1 when bought in bulk, but if selected individually by the collector choice cards can cost as much as £1 each. My collection includes many postcards with a photographic theme.

Carte-de-visite of my father as a child 1895.

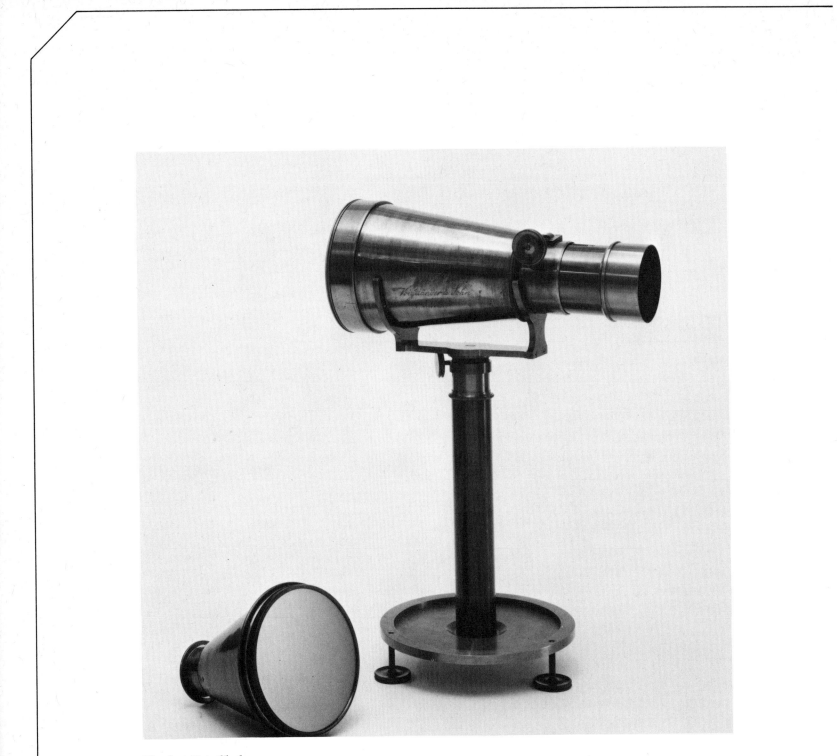

The first Voigtländer daguerreotype camera 1840. Courtesy of The Science Museum.

Note: the three leveling screws on base plate have gotten put in upside down! -RLB

EARLIEST CAMERAS

MOST of the cameras and apparatus used by the pioneer photographers are now carefully preserved in museums. The world's first photograph, a view from his window at Gras taken on a bitumen-coated pewter plate by Niépce in France in the summer of 1827, was brought to light by Helmut and Alison Gernsheim in England in January 1952, and is now in the Gernsheim collection at the University of Texas, USA. Several of Niépce's cameras are in the Musée Denon at Chalon-sur-Saône, France, including one, possibly the earliest, which is a typical sliding box camera of the period. Some of the cameras used by Talbot are in the collections of the Royal Photographic Society and the Science Museum in London. Occasionally, an early item comes to light, but such articles are very rare and valuable. At an auction at the Parke-Bernet Galleries in New York on 7th February 1970, a half-plate daguerreotype camera made in 1852, measuring $7'' \times 8\frac{3}{4}'' \times 12''$, fitted with a Voigtländer lens No. 4417 and complete on a tripod of the same period, was sold for $2,600 (£1,030). This however is hardly a typical price that the average collector has to pay as I have recently purchased a whole-plate sliding box daguerreotype camera of about the same period for £10 and, some while ago, I bought a quarter-plate sliding box camera made in the 1850s for £3.50 ($8) in a London market.

The photographic process invented by Daguerre was the one which proved most practical and became financially successful, dominating the first decade of photography. The images, apparatus and literature associated with this process were the first to be produced in any considerable quantity, and are the ones most likely to be found by collectors.

Daguerreotypes are easily recognizable. They are highly polished, silver-plated sheets of copper (a very small number were made on solid silver plates), with a mirror-like surface, and they must be held at just the correct angle to the light for their delicately detailed images to be seen. Covered with a gilt mat and a piece of glass and the whole bound together with tape to prevent air or dust from reaching the photograph, they were usually placed in a small case or frame. After all this time (the process flourished from 1839 until the 1850s) many that are found now show signs of oxidization or are in otherwise poor condition. They can be restored and the tarnish removed providing that the image itself has not been damaged but I personally feel that unless the daguerreotype has tarnished so badly that the image cannot be seen it should not be

Joseph Nicéphore Niépce who took the world's first successful photograph in 1827.

(Right) Taken on a pewter plate by Nicéphore Niépce, 1826 and re-photographed from the television screen during the showing of the B.B.C. 2 Collector's World programme 'The Victorian Image – Photography' February 1972; this image brings together the oldest and newest methods of photography.

Sliding box daguerreotype camera made by Lerebours et Secretan, Paris 1844.

touched. In my opinion completely restored daguerreotypes often lose that elegant air of age which can so enhance their value and beauty.

Prices of daguerreotypes, like so many other examples of early Victoriana can vary enormously, depending often as much on the place of purchase, as on condition, size or rarity. Small ones can be bought for a pound or two, whilst only a little while ago I paid £10 ($25) for a quarter-plate daguerreotype in a lovely papiermâché case inlaid with mother of pearl. On the other hand at the auction of the Will Weissberg Collection of Rare Photographs, Cameras, and Related Devices at the Parke-Bernet Galleries in New York on 16th May 1967 two nude stereoscopic daguerreotypes were sold for $150 (approximately £60) each; and at a similar sale at the same venue on 7th February 1970 an item from the Sidney Strober Collection, a large group portrait of fifteen girls and three instructors from the Rutgers Female Institute taken on a horizontal mammoth-sized daguerreotype plate measuring $11'' \times 14''$, was sold for $300 (£120). Because of the very long exposures then necessary the earliest photographs were all views or still life subjects, but these are now very rare and almost all the daguerreotypes that are found by collectors are portraits.

The daguerreotype process soon proved to be a blind alley. Not only were daguerreotypes difficult to see because of their mirror-like surface, but they also had the great disadvantage that each was an individual image and was not readily reproducible. In Europe the process died away soon after the death of Daguerre himself in 1851, but not without leaving behind a wealth of photographs and artefacts for collectors.

The improved calotype process that had been patented by Fox Talbot in 1841 produced a paper negative from which an almost unlimited number of positive prints

Miss Dorothy Catherine Draper taken by her brother Professor John William Draper M.D., LL.D., of the University of the City of New York, early in 1840. This was one of the first daguerreotype portraits ever made. Six minutes exposure was given.

could be made and was the direct ancestor of the negative-positive process used today. Because the paper used could not reproduce the fine details possible with metal plates, and also because of Fox Talbot's stringent patents, it never attained the popularity of the daguerreotype, and examples are now very rare and much sought after by collectors.

In 1848, Abel Niépce de Saint-Victor, who was Nicéphore Niépce's cousin, published his method of applying albumen to glass plates. The albumen-coated plate was sensitized with nitrate of silver, and developed after exposure with gallic acid. These albumen plates produced much finer detail than was possible with calotype paper, and like them, gave a reproducible negative image. They were not suitable for portraits because, with the lenses then available, they were painfully slow needing even in good light at least five or ten minutes exposure. This, however, was of little consequence when taking landscape or still life photographs, and they were much used for reproducing works of art. Albumen positives

Metal daguerreotype camera made by Thomas Davidson 1842. Courtesy of The Royal Scottish Museum.

One of Fox Talbot's calotype cameras with a calotype and apparatus. The heated iron was used for spreading the wax on paper negatives to make them more transparent, from the Fox talbot relics at Lacock Abbey. Courtesy of The Royal Scottish Museum.

were perfect for stereoscopic and lantern slides and were extensively used in the 1850s and 1860s by such famous photographers as Ferrier in France and the Langenheim Brothers in America. Ferrier's slides were made in such large numbers that, although they were of the finest quality, even perfect examples are of no great value today. By way of contrast, examples of the earliest Langenheim stereo slides made in 1854 have recently changed hands amongst collectors in America for $100 (£40) each.

These processes were all superseded by the wet collodion process, invented in England by Frederick Scott Archer in 1851. The glass plate was coated with collodion (a solution of gun-cotton in ether) and the film formed on the glass was sensitized with a solution of silver nitrate. It was then immediately exposed and processed while still wet. As all this manipulation had to be done when the photograph was taken, a photographer leaving his studio behind had

William Henry Fox Talbot F.R.S. with one of his cameras 1864.

Large daguerreotype camera used by Fox Talbot. Courtesy of The Royal Scottish Museum.

to take a portable dark room with him, and had to be a cross between a conjurer and a strong man! The high quality and shorter exposure time of the wet plate made it worthwhile however, and the collodion wet plate dominated photography for almost thirty years.

Anything associated with this early part of the history of photography is treasured by collectors. As well as the cameras used by these pioneer photographers and the images that they produced, such items as daguerreotype buffing boards and fuming boxes, the chemical bottles and tanks used in the wet collodion process, plate boxes, portable dark tents, and all the para-

phernalia of the period should also be sought after to help round out a collection and add to its interest.

Two different types of photographs were produced from the wet collodion negatives. Processed normally, they could be used to produce paper prints—usually on paper coated with sensitized albumen. If however they were processed to produce a lighter negative, and then placed on a dark surface, they appeared to be positive images. With the back lacquered black or brown, or placed on a piece of dark velvet, these new photographs were bound in glass and sold in the same types of frames and cases that had been used for the daguerreotypes. They were much cheaper than daguerreotypes, and became from about 1852 the most popular form of photography until the carte-de-visite photograph became fashionable in the early 1860s. Although Scott Archer had allowed free use of his invention, it was patented in America in 1854 by James A. Cutting of Boston. It is said that Cutting's friend Marcus A. Root, a 'Daguerrian Artist', first suggested the name ambrotype by which they were popularly known. Collectors will discover that the same cameras were often used for all of these early processes. It was no problem to use wet collodion plates in a daguerreotype camera, and the plate holder of a wet plate camera was easily adapted to take tintypes. I have in my collection two sliding box cameras from the early 1860s that were used by two generations of street photographers. The cameras were used in turn for wet collodion plates, tintypes, and dry plates with only slight modifications to the slide holders. The slide holders used with wet collodion plates are easily identified. They usually had silver wire reinforcement across the corners as the glue used would not hold when wet. They can also be recognized by the groove at the bottom for draining away surplus liquid, and by the black stains caused by the silver salts used to sensitize the emulsion.

Daguerreotypes and ambrotypes can be found in many sizes, and many different types of cases and frames. The size most often found today is the one-sixth-plate ($2\frac{3}{4}'' \times 3\frac{1}{4}''$) which was the most popular. Many other sizes were made from the one-sixteenth-plate ($1\frac{3}{8}'' \times 1\frac{5}{8}''$)—and the even smaller sizes used in jewellery—to the $13'' \times 14''$ giants that were made by Antoine Claudet in 1843 using his new Petzval portrait lens. At first, the smaller daguerreotypes and ambrotypes were usually sold in wooden cases covered with fine morocco leather and lined with plush, similar to those used for miniature portraits. From 1854 to 1861, the Union case, patented in the United States in October 1854 by Samuel Peck of New Haven, Connecticut, was widely used. It was made of the first thermo-plastic, a mixture of shellac and papiermâché or other fibrous material which became plastic when heated, so that it could be pressed into a mould or between dies. Usually black or brown, a small number were made in light colours, and a few only were made in two colours. These rare ones are highly prized by collectors.

A specialized collection of the cases used to protect daguerreotypes and ambrotypes, which could be divided into sections such as 'leather' cases, 'Union' cases, 'decorated' cases, 'named' cases (cases marked with the name of the maker, or more rarely that of the photographer), would be of great interest, and for collectors with limited space and income at their disposal, it would have the added attraction of being compact and comparatively inexpensive. A book, *American Miniature Case Art* by Floyd and Marion Rinhart, published by A.S. Barnes and Company Incorporated in the United States in 1969, is devoted to this subject, and will be of great interest to collectors.

The budding collector will find that ambrotype portraits are the easiest early photographs to find. By the 1850s there were more and more professional photographers in business, from those who catered for the wealthy and charged many guineas for a sitting, to those who charged 3d. or 6d. for a portrait with the added inducement of a free gift such as a shoe shine or a rasher of bacon for each customer. One interesting variation of the ambrotype was the relievo which appeared in 1854. To make this, only the portrait and the studio props were backed with dark paint or varnish, and the rest of the picture was erased. A thick piece of glass was placed between the ambrotype and a light coloured background, giving a three dimensional effect to the two dimensional image. This was an attempt to cash in on the great upsurge of interest in stereoscopic photography which came at this time.

Tintype photographs, taken on lacquered or tinned iron plates, were another version of this process. Patented in the United States in February 1856, and in England in December of that year, they had actually originated in France, where they had been described by E.A. Martin in 1853. Known first as melainotype or ferrotype photographs, the name tintype—possibly because of their cheap tinny look—soon came into

Family of a street photographer in London 1910, showing two portable dark rooms, and a half plate sliding box camera, 1860. This photograph was taken with a similar camera.

Tintype photograph of a family group on the porch of their house.

The photographs on these Cartes-de-Visite show how for the first time the public began to know what famous people really looked like

GARIBALDI.
(From Life.)

PARNELL

DÉLIÉ   6. B.^d des Italiens

The Right Hon. W. E. Gladstone, M. P.

ALFRED TENNYSON

The reverse side of cartes-de-visite were usually used to advertise the photographer and many had amusing engravings showing photographic studios of the day. The U.S. revenue stamp on the back of the card by Harter of Auburn, New York helps to date the photograph as this was a tax imposed on photographs during the American Civil War

popular use, and this is the name by which they are known to collectors today. They were first sold in the same cases as daguerreotypes and ambrotypes and, as with the earlier photographs, small examples were used in brooches and lockets. However, they were soon only being made by the cheapest of the photographers who put them into card or paper cases.

Tintypes achieved great popularity in the United States in the 1860s, and collectable examples can still be found. During the Civil War, soldiers in both the Union and the Confederate armies liked them because they were relatively inexpensive, and could be mailed home in a letter with little risk of breakage. Although large numbers were made they are getting progressively more difficult to discover. Any Civil War period photographs should be treasured. They are

being sought, not only by collectors, but also by those who are interested in the Civil War itself, military matters in general, or in that specific period of American history, and original photographs of that time are rapidly becoming rare. Tintypes did not come into general use in Great Britain and Europe until the 1880s, when they became known as 'American' while-you-wait photographs, and they are still being made and sold at fairgrounds and racetracks today.

The typical sepia colouring will help collectors to identify many of the paper prints of the wet collodion plate period. Wet collodion negatives were printed by sunlight on paper which had been coated with a fine film of albumen (the white of eggs), and then sensitized. After printing it was fixed and toned. Examples of the carte-de-visite which became so very popular in the early 1860s, are easily found. As the name suggests, these were paper prints pasted on to card mounts the size of the standard visiting card ($4'' \times 2\frac{1}{2}''$). Claudet had shown a multiplying camera with a repeating back (a movable plate holder) at the Great Exhibition in London in 1851. This had made it possible to take a series of small

pictures on a large wet plate, and it was soon adapted for taking carte-de-visite photographs. The carte-de-visite was patented by Andre Adolph Eugene Disderi in 1854, but it was not until Disderi took carte-de-visite photographs of the Emperor Napoleon III in May 1859 that they became really popular. Repeating backs were used on single lens, binocular, and multiple lens cameras, and a rich medley of both the images themselves and the apparatus used for their production lies waiting for the collector. The first carte-de-visite photographs were small close-up portraits showing only the head and shoulders of the sitter, but full length photographs were soon taken. Faces on these were so small that retouching was unnecessary, cutting out one stage in their production, and making them even more profitable to the photographer.

In 1866, another new size was introduced to replace the fading public interest in the carte-de-visite. This was the cabinet size, a $5\frac{1}{2}'' \times 4''$ photograph pasted in to a $6\frac{1}{2}'' \times 4\frac{1}{2}''$ mount. Although many other sizes were made, these two remained the most popular professional sizes until the

Carte-de-visite photographs from a Japanese album 1865.

early cameras and their accessories.

The collection should include some examples of the photograph albums in use at that time. Almost every family had an album of some sort, filled with photographs, not only of the family and friends, but also of notables such as royalty, leading politicians, clergy and the like. It was possible to determine a man's opinions by observing the politicians and clergymen that he displayed in his albums.

Some of these albums were plain and severe, indeed some were very cheap and shoddy; but for the collector there are albums with elaborate and beautiful covers, decorative surrounds to the photographs, and some with a music box enclosed in the back, which plays a tinkling tune when the album is picked up.

The cards on which these carte-de-visite and cabinet size photographs were mounted usually carried a printed advertisement for the photographer, sometimes on the front of the card, but more often on the back. A selection of these in a collection would help to illustrate the times in which they were made, and give some idea of the cost and status of photography in those days.

early part of the twentieth century.

Even at this early stage in the evolution of photography, the necessity for the collector to specialize can be clearly seen; and the successful collector will be the one who seeks out a corner of this vast field that is to his particular liking, and sticks to it. Once a collector defines his field his next task is to make sure his collection is kept in an orderly manner, with a proper catalogue or file, or the whole idea will soon tend to get out of hand, and what should be an enjoyable and well-cared-for collection, will become a jumble of odds and ends. Specialization and documentation are the essentials of all collecting, and are particularly necessary when dealing with bulky things like

Camera obscuras, daguerreotype and wet plate cameras, and indeed any item of equipment from those early days should be treasured by the collector, as they are now of great historical interest. These cameras from the dawn of photography were not produced as cameras are today. A production of a few thousand would have been considered a very good run for a popular camera, compared with millions that are turned out today, and finds of these early items will be few and far between. Although some collectors may be luckier than others in this respect, it should be remembered that although photography is young in years, cameras are fragile.

Folding camera for paper
negatives made by Marcus
Sparling, 1854.

Mahogany sliding box
camera with petzval type
lens by Lerebours et Secretan
of Paris, 1855, sold for £840
($1932) at Christies on 25th
April 1974. Courtesy of
Christies.

This smaller mahogany sliding
box camera which is a later
example of this type of camera
– the rapid rectilinear lens has
provision for Waterhouse stops
– brought £420 ($966) at
Christies on 25th April 1974.
Courtesy of Christies.

Half plate mahogany sliding
box camera 1858.

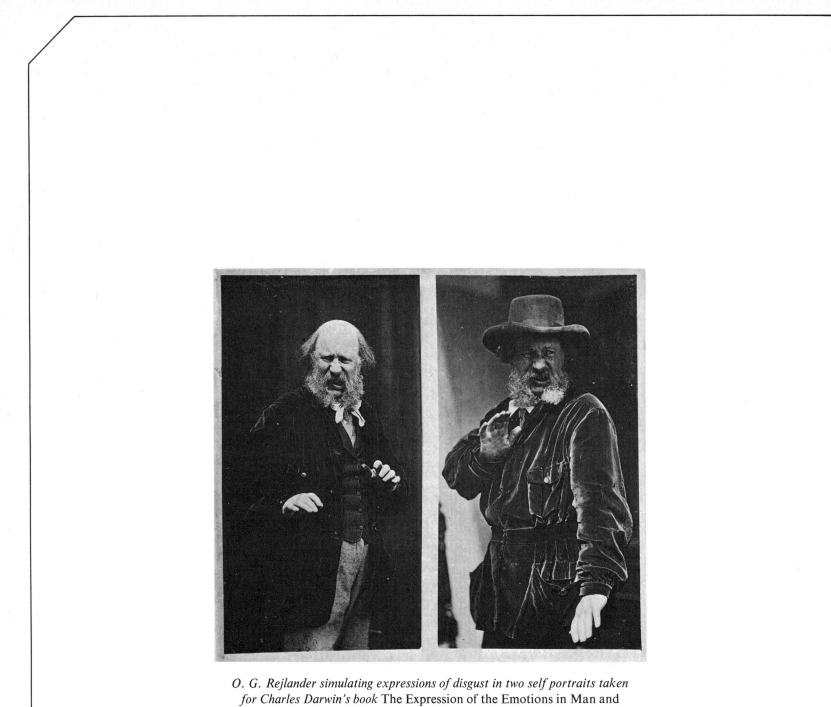

O. G. Rejlander simulating expressions of disgust in two self portraits taken for Charles Darwin's book The Expression of the Emotions in Man and Animals. *London 1872.*

EARLY DRY PLATE AND ROLL FILM CAMERAS

CAMERA collecting really gets into its stride with the new crop of cameras that were produced in the 1880s to take advantage of the then recently perfected gelatine dry plate process. Serious collectors will delight in the imaginative new designs that became available, examples of many of which can still be found today. The new process brought with it new instruction manuals, new apparatus, and a host of new items of ephemera which are becoming more and more collectable with the passage of time. The gelatine dry plate was a British invention, as were so many of the innovations of those days, and was first described in the *British Journal of Photography* by Dr Richard Leach Maddox in 1871. It was faster and easier to use than any of the earlier processes and was the first step towards the modern system of professional developing and printing.

Collectors will realize that wet plate photography was not for the feeble. The photographer had to be part scientist, part technician and part strong man. He had to work next to his dark room, or take a portable one—complete with bottles of distilled water, chemicals and heavy glass plates—with him wherever he went with his great cumbersome camera and its solid stand or tripod. Outfits of this kind can still be seen at museums, and make a wonderful addition to any collection. Wet collodion plates had to be prepared immediately before use, and developed while they were still wet. Dry plates however could be purchased ready for use, stored if necessary, and developed at a convenient time after exposure. It was soon discovered that boiling or stewing the emulsion before coating these new plates, greatly increased its speed. This meant that it was no longer

Wet plate landscape photographer with 'portable' dark tent outfit.

The fishing boat, by Frank M. Sutcliffe.

necessary for the photographer to use a camera stand or tripod.

Among serious photographers of this period there was a search for new photographic ideas and images, and a turning away from the contrived work and studio portraits that had dominated the art for so many years. For the collector, a showcase comparing the work of early photographers such as Oscar Gustave Rejlander or Henry Peach Robinson, with examples of the output of some of the new wave of photographers, men like Dr Peter Henry Emerson (an American amateur photographer living in London) or Frank Meadow Sutcliffe, a professional photographer, would illustrate the changed outlook that these new cameras and dry plates brought to the photographer.

Dry plate and photographic equipment were designed to appeal to all sections of the populace. Boys' outfits, ladies' outfits, cameras for beginners, advanced amateurs and professional photographers proliferated. New models were brought out to take advantage of each innovation and improvement in sensitized material and lenses, all unknowingly adding to the great store of apparatus that can now be found by the enthusiastic collector.

By the mid-1880s an exciting burst of creativity was producing a vast variety of hand cameras which are now highly valued by collectors. They were much smaller and lighter than the unwieldy wet plate cameras that they replaced and, although they were made in many sizes, the most popular were the quarter-plate ($3\frac{1}{4}'' \times 4\frac{1}{4}''$). Simple sliding or flap shutters, or just the removal of the lens cap, had sufficed to expose wet plates but this new breed of cameras was equipped with instantaneous shutters, and the novel types of shutters that were developed, were intriguing.

Before the introduction of dry plates, the paraphernalia and preparations necessary when a photograph was taken made the intention of the photographer only too obvious. The new hand held dry plate cameras could be used easily and simply without all the fuss and bother that had accompanied the earlier photographic processes, and they became known as 'detective' cameras. An advertisement for Schmid's Patent Detective Camera in 1884 read 'anyone provided with this instrument can take photographs while walking along the street without attracting notice from the curious', and others soon pointed out the advantage of being able to take 'surreptitious negatives'.

Many of these new cameras were disguised as everyday objects, or designed so as to be easily concealed about the person of the photographer. They were very popular and it became the fashion to carry a detective camera. To quote from *The A.B.C. of Photography*, published by the London Stereoscopic Company in 1889, 'The disguises of the detective camera are various and their name is legion, silk hats, hand-bags, dummy babies, dispatch cases, picnic baskets, parcels of books, single volumes, opera glasses, and even baskets of flowers have in turn sheltered cameras.'

The first detective cameras were large wooden boxes made to look like workmen's tool boxes. Fallowfield's Facile was a typical example, and it was often wrapped in brown paper and string to further disguise it. It was manufactured in small numbers, even the popular lines being made in hundreds rather than thousands. Consequently, specimens are now very rare. Connoisseurs will treasure them as much as the later more unusual and imaginative models, and collectors everywhere are searching, for instance, for examples of Stirn's Waistcoat Detective Camera which was made in 1886. Shaped like a circular metal plate 6″ in diameter and 1″ thick, with a protruding lens, it was suspended around the neck on a strap, and worn concealed under the waistcoat. The black lens housing came through one of the buttonholes in lieu of the button, which it closely resembled. A larger size was also made and this seems to be much rarer. It measured 7″ in diameter and made four circular $2\frac{1}{2}$″ diameter negatives on a $6\frac{3}{4}$″ diameter plate. One of these larger models was sold for £420 ($966) at Sotheby's in January 1975.

Small hand detective cameras that looked like binocular or monocular field glasses were made by many manufacturers. Several of these took photographs at right angles to the direction in which they were apparently pointed, the shutter release opening a small port in the side to reveal the lens immediately before the exposure. Although not made in any great quantity, cameras of this type were being sold right up to the 1920s. One most unusual detective camera in my collection is built into a leather binocular case. When the catch on the cover of the case is pressed, it moves a small flap of leather at one end uncovering the lens and then releases the shutter. It is fitted with a magazine holding six $1\frac{3}{4}$″ × $2\frac{3}{8}$″ plates.

By the turn of the century many types of change box cameras were being made. The change box, which fitted onto the back of the camera, held the plates (usually twelve) and after each exposure the front plate was lifted out and placed at the back by means of a soft leather or cloth bag which was attached to the box. This allowed the plates to be changed in daylight. One adventurous change box camera that collectors will relish was the Nydia, made by Newman and Guardia Limited of London, in 1893. A quarter-plate camera weighing only one pound, it was fitted with a Wray $5\frac{1}{2}$″ rapid rectilinear lens and a pneumatic shutter. Sold successfully for six years, it was replaced by an improved version in 1900. This new Nydia, made of mahogany with black bronzed brass and German silver metal parts, had a swing back, and could be purchased with a changing box for either twelve cut films, or eight plates.

Pocketability was always a desirable attribute in cameras and collectors will find early examples of this in the Xit cameras introduced in the 1890s by J.F. Shew and Company, of Newman Street, London. The Xit was made in so many variations that they are the collectors' delight.

Another kind of camera that began to be produced at about the same time in large quantities was the magazine camera.

J. Lancaster and Sons quarter plate Le Marveillux sold by Benetfink and Co., London 1890.

Adam's and Co.'s Presto detective or hand camera 1890. This simple camera is now a prized collector's item.

Lancaster's patent watch camera 1890.

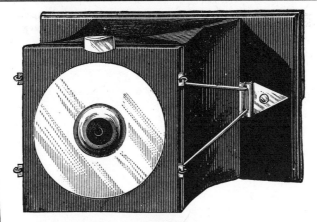

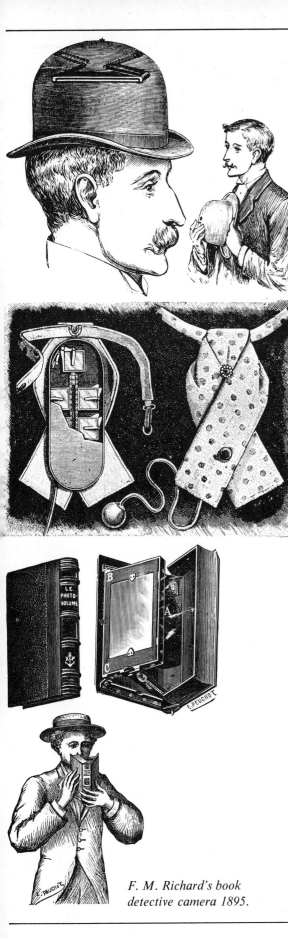

Adam's and Co.'s 'Hat' detective camera, 1891.

"If they knew what I wore when I walked in the street,
  I would be quite a terror to the people I meet.
They'd fly when they saw me, and not stop to chat,
  For I carry a camera inside my hat!"

Lady's purse detective camera 1891.

The 'Photo-cravate'. E. Block's necktie detective camera, 1890. One of these cameras (without the cravate) was sold for £1,600 ($4,000) at Sotheby's on 21st June 1974.

J. Lancaster and Sons Le Merveilleux quarter plate pocket camera 1888.

F. M. Richard's book detective camera 1895.

Jonathan Fallowfield's Facile quarter plate detective camera 1889.

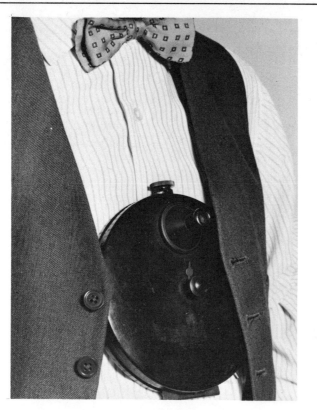

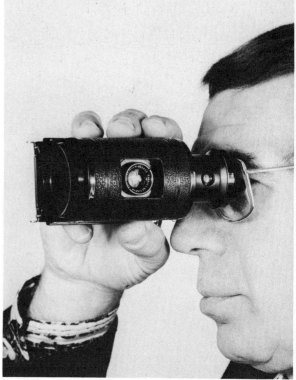

The Ergo monocular camera using a 4.5×6 cm film pack was made by Contessa Nettel in Germany between 1919 when these two firms joined together, and 1926 when they became part of the great Zeiss Ikon combine. Two versions were made one with a circular and the other with a rectangular opening which were uncovered by a light pressure on the shutter release, revealing the lens.

Stirns detective camera 1886, was worn under the waistcoat with the lens protruding through a buttonhole in place of one of the buttons. One was sold for £620 ($1550) at Sotheby's on 21st June 1974.

This held twelve or more plates (later models took cut films) and although outwardly the black boxes look much alike, an interesting exhibition could be arranged to show the many different methods used to bring the plates into position. The Gaumont Jumelle was made in a style that was popular in France at the end of the 1890s. They can still be occasionally found there by collectors but they are extremely rare in the British Isles.

The Frena, made by R. and J. Beck of 68, Cornhill, in the City of London, was a much more unusual magazine camera and is much more interesting to the collector. Taking forty flat films at a loading, it dealt them one by one, 'like a pack of cards', at the turn of a handle. Five models of the Frena were advertised in 1899 and a complete set would look fine in any collection of cameras. Although I have been unable to unearth any reliable data as to the exact numbers of each of the various models of the Frena that were produced, most of those that I have seen in collections are examples

of the smaller and less expensive models, the larger sizes being relatively rare.

Photography's next great leap forward was in 1888, when George Eastman introduced his original Kodak roll film camera, and once again a fresh flood of collectable cameras appeared.

Roll films of various kinds, and roll-film cameras and holders—of great interest to the collector—had been produced before this but it was the Eastman Kodak box camera that brought about the great expansion of photography that really made it possible for everyone to have a camera.

In 1855 Eastman had introduced the Eastman-Walker roll holder, which could be used instead of a dark slide on almost any camera. Roller slides were not a new idea. The first patent had been taken out by Spencer and Melhuish in England in 1854 for one that used a calotype paper, but it was not produced in any quantity. Although there are still Eastman-Walker roll holders about I don't know of any collector who has an example of the original Spencer-Melhuish one.

George Eastman built up a thriving business, always striving to develop new ideas and materials. By putting many of these ideas together he created the Kodak camera. The original Kodak of 1888 was designed to be 'the smallest, lightest, and simplest of all detective cameras', and it fulfilled all the claims that were made for it. Tens of thousands of these Kodaks were made but they are now extremely rare. In almost twenty years of collecting I have not been able to find one. This very first Kodak, which was made in the Rochester factory of the Eastman Dry Plate and Film Company, was a fixed focus box camera. It had an *f* 8 lens giving sharp pictures of everything more than 8′ away, and a cylindrical shutter.

Although the camera could hold enough film for 150 circular photographs $2\frac{1}{2}''$ in diameter, it was usually sold loaded for a hundred exposures. After the film had been exposed, the camera was returned to the factory where the pictures were developed and printed, and the camera reloaded with a fresh roll of film. At long last the photographer was completely free of the dark room and its burdensome activities, and could devote himself (or herself) entirely to the art of taking pictures. George Eastman wrote in the Kodak instruction manual: 'There are only three simple operations, 1. Pull the string (to set the shutter). 2. Turn the key (to put fresh film into position). 3. Press the button (to make the exposure).' It was the proud Kodak boast 'You press the button—we do the rest!'

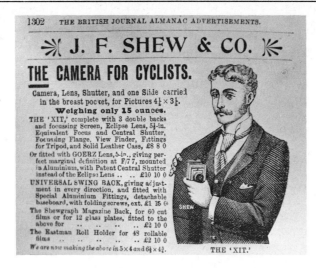

These first Kodaks used Eastman paper stripping film (paper being used as a support for the sensitized gelatine emulsion) but in the following year a nitro-cellulose film was introduced and a second model of the Kodak was produced which had a reciprocating shutter, but was otherwise similar to the original model. This 1889 version of the Kodak was also called the No. 1 Kodak. The No. 2 Kodak, taking 100 $3\frac{1}{2}''$ circular pictures, was marketed soon afterwards.

No exact figures for the production runs of these earliest Kodaks are available. Large numbers were made but the film for them was discontinued in 1900. As a result of this, very few have survived until today. I have found several specimens of the second and third generation Kodaks in the past, but they too are becoming more and more scarce. Collectors can see examples of almost all of the early Kodaks in the Kodak Museum at Harrow, but very few—if any— private collectors can boast of having a comprehensive selection of their own. Others have laid claims to the invention of the name Kodak and of the camera, but these claims have never been substantiated. Research has always confirmed that the Kodak was George Eastman's.

Before the end of 1890, the No. 3 Regular Kodak taking 250 pictures, $3\frac{1}{4}'' \times 4\frac{1}{4}''$, the No. 4 Regular Kodak taking 250 pictures, $4'' \times 5''$, and the No. 4 Kodak Junior which took forty-eight pictures, $4'' \times 5''$, were being produced and the first folding Kodak camera was introduced.

In 1891, the first Daylight Kodaks were marketed. The model 'A' took twenty-four pictures, $2\frac{3}{4}'' \times 3\frac{1}{4}''$, the model 'B' twenty-four pictures, $3\frac{1}{2}'' \times 4''$, and the model 'C' twenty-four pictures, $4'' \times 5''$. Although these cameras were called Daylight Kodaks it was recommended that the celluloid film, even though it was protected by black paper leaders and trailers, be only loaded indoors, or at night.

It was not until the cartridge type of roll film was introduced in 1895 that a camera could be loaded in broad daylight. The first cameras to use this new system were the No. 2 Bullet, the No. 2 Bull's Eye, both box cameras taking eighteen pictures, $3\frac{1}{2}'' \times 3\frac{1}{2}''$, and equipped with a fixed focus single achromatic lens with three stops, and also the Pocket Kodak. This, the first Kodak to be made partly of aluminium, was equipped with a fixed focus lens with three stops and an automatic time and instantaneous shutter, measured only $2\frac{3}{4}'' \times 2\frac{7}{8}'' \times 3\frac{7}{8}''$, and was the first of the really small roll film cameras. Taking twelve pictures, $1\frac{1}{2}'' \times 2''$, collectors can identify the earliest version by the circular field of the viewfinder, later models having a rectangular viewfinder and a rotary shutter. These Pocket Kodaks could also be used with plates instead of roll films. A strip of film covered by a slightly longer strip of black paper was wrapped around a flanged spool to make the lightproof cartridge used in these cameras.

The first of many Folding Pocket Kodaks was the No. 1, introduced in 1897. The first with an all-metal case, it measured just over $1\frac{1}{2}'' \times 3\frac{1}{2}'' \times 6\frac{1}{2}''$, and took twelve $2\frac{1}{4}'' \times 3\frac{1}{4}''$ exposures. This was to become a standard size negative for roll film cameras,

J. F. Shew and Co.'s Aluminium Xit folding camera 1899.

The 9 × 12cm Gaumont Jumelle 1899, is a typical French camera of the period.

Eastman's roll holder was introduced in 1885.

and collectors should treasure this model as most modern roll film cameras are descended from it. It was followed in quick succession in 1899 by the No. 2 Folding Pocket Kodak taking twelve $3\frac{1}{2}'' \times 3\frac{1}{2}''$ negatives, and in 1900 by the No. 1a taking $2\frac{1}{4}'' \times 4\frac{1}{4}''$ negatives, and the No. 3 taking $3\frac{1}{4}'' \times 4\frac{1}{4}''$ negatives. Many other Folding Pocket Kodaks were produced over the years as improved shutters and lenses came on the market. When we consider the large numbers of Kodaks that were sold, it is surprising that there are not even more of them about today.

At an early stage in his collecting career, the budding collector will have to make up his mind what he is going to do about box cameras in general, and the run-of-the-mill folding Kodaks in particular. Unless, as some of my friends have done, you intend to make a specific collection of box cameras, or concentrate on collecting Kodaks only, you will find that your collection is flooded with these types of cameras which were made by the millions. There are of course many interesting examples of both these types of cameras which would be an asset to any collection, but my feeling is that only the earlier or more unusual models are worth keeping. The outstanding collector of box cameras is Eaton S. Lothrop, Jr., who has a remark-able collection of many hundreds of early and unusual models.

A variety of shapes, colours and sizes puts life into a collection of any kind and this is especially true of a display of early cameras. If you are going to collect box cameras, or folding Kodaks, you must keep a look out for examples of the many different coloured ones that were made, as well as for the more exotic and technically exciting models that are usually collected. The Vanity Vest Pocket Kodak model III of 1928, is a typical coloured folding camera, and was made in blue, brown, grey, green and red.

In 1914, Kodak paid $300,000 to H.J. Gaisman for the rights to the Autographic system he had invented, which made it possible for the photographer to write information and names directly onto the film at the time of exposure. This was an enormous amount of money in those days and very large numbers of Autographic Kodaks were produced from 1914 until this feature was discontinued in 1934.

So many Autographic Kodaks were sold that most collectors ignore them as having little if any interest, and no value. However, as with most Kodak cameras, each model was made in several versions, and could be fitted with almost any suitable lens and shutter. Examples with Zeiss tessar lenses and compur shutters are amongst the more unusual ones that are collected.

From the early days Kodak provided an upgrading service for their cameras. For fairly moderate charges, lenses could be exchanged for better ones, shutters could be replaced with superior types, and camera backs could be converted to Autographics. This is why collectors find many varieties of Kodaks which are not listed by the manufacturers. Because of this practice of changing camera backs, collectors should not

The No. 1 Kodak camera of 1888. The camera that brought snapshooting to the man in the street. Courtesy of The Kodak Museum.

The 'B' Ordinary Kodak (The 'A' Ordinary Kodak had no viewfinder, and the 'C' Ordinary Kodak had two viewfinders, they were all made in Rochester, U.S.A. 1892).

No. 1 Folding Pocket Kodak 1898, one early advertisement for this camera reads:– "Folds with a nod, opens with a touch, and is eminently suitable for cyclists" Courtesy of The Kodak Museum.

The No. 1A Speed Kodak 1909 was fitted with a multiple slit Graphlex focal plane shutter with speeds up to 1/1000 second.

place too much reliance on the patent dates engraved in them when estimating the ages of cameras.

Another Kodak 'first' worth looking out for, is the No. 3a Autographic Special. Introduced in 1916, it was the first camera with a coupled rangefinder. Taking $3\frac{1}{4}'' \times 5\frac{1}{2}''$ pictures, it was fitted with a variety of lenses and shutters. Typical perhaps was the model fitted with a Kodak anastigmat $f6·3$ lens in a Velosto shutter, which cost £16 ($64) and one lovely model which had a Zeiss $f6·3$ anastigmat lens in a compur shutter. With a little luck the collector will find an example of the No. 1a Autographic Special, taking $2\frac{1}{2}'' \times 4\frac{1}{4}''$ pictures, which was also fitted with the Kodak coupled range-finder and was produced in 1920. Although this coupled rangefinder was not easy to use successfully, it was the first of its kind and therefore of great value in a collection pointing the way as it did, towards future developments. These cameras could be included in a collection of Kodak cameras, or kept with a specialized collection showing the development of coupled rangefinder cameras.

The history of photography for the past eighty years has to a considerable extent been bound up with the history of Kodak and a specialized collection of Kodak cameras would show many of the great advances that were made in photography during this period. Although large numbers of Kodak cameras have been made, it is, as always, the earlier and more unusual models and varieties that should be looked for and treasured when found. These are the irreplaceable ones, which will one day become as rare and valuable as daguerreo-type and wet plate cameras are today.

There are several publications which are of great help to Kodak enthusiasts. The *Kodak Collector* published in 1972 by Alan R. Feinberg (PO Box 27, Winnetka, Illinois, 60093, USA) lists most of the Kodak

The Kodak Girl

The Kodak Girl 1914.

Business card of the Rochester Optical Company.

and Brownie cameras made from 1888 until the 1960s giving particulars of lenses, shutters, film sizes, picture sizes, prices and dates of manufacture etc.; Classic Photo-graphic Apparatus of Simsbury, Con-necticut, USA, published a *Special* 1972 *Reprint Edition of the 1894 Kodak Catalogue* which contains details and illustrations of many of the Kodak and Kodet cameras of that time; and the *Catalogue of the Kodak*

type has been made by Kodak.

Although Beard had sold 'coloured' daguerreotypes as early as 1842—and many collectors will have examples of these tinted daguerreotypes as they are fairly common, having been made in large numbers—real colour photography originated with the work of James Clerk Maxwell, who suggested making separation negatives in a communication to the Royal Society of Edinburgh in 1855. Working with Dr Thomas Sutton, an expert photographer, he produced the three now famous separation negatives made through red, green and blue filters, of a piece of tartan ribbon on a black velvet background. Projecting positive transparencies made from these negatives through a similar set of filters fitted to three magic lanterns, Maxwell showed his first coloured picture at the Royal Society on 17th May 1861. The negatives used in this experiment are now in the collection of the Cavendish Laboratory, Cambridge.

This was the first example of the additive method of colour reproduction that was later to be used by Frederic E. Ives in his Kromscop projecting and viewing devices in 1892.

7th May 1869 saw another of the great coincidences in the history of photography. At a meeting of the Societé Française de Photographie two sealed letters were opened and read. Acting separately, and without knowledge of each other or of Maxwell's work, both Charles Cros and Louis Ducos du Hauron announced methods of making coloured photographs using three negatives taken through coloured filters. It was Ducos du Hauron however who successfully carried on the work, and in 1874 he patented a camera for making three or more separation negatives for colour photography.

It is from this date onwards that collectable apparatus begins to appear, and any of the early one shot, tri-colour, repeat-

Museum, Harrow, Middlesex, England, which was published in 1947, is a real mine of invaluable information. Although out of print for many years now, copies still come to hand. One was listed for $12.50 (£5) in the Spring 1972 issue of the *Daguerrian Era Catalogue of Photographic Antiques and Literature*, published by the Daguerrian Era (Tom and Elinor Burnside of Vermont, USA), which made it a collectors' item itself.

One of the more uncommon Kodak cameras in my collection is a one shot tri-colour roll film box camera. It carries no identification other than the injunction 'Use Kodak Film', inscribed on the winding key. Taking three simultaneous $2\frac{1}{4}'' \times 3\frac{1}{4}''$ pictures through blue, green and red filters respectively, on 620 roll film, it is a simplified version of the colour cameras that were used for half a century. This camera must have been made privately as, although it is made of Kodak parts, no camera of this

The No. 3A Autographic Kodak Special made in Rochester, U.S.A., was the first camera to have a coupled rangefinder, 1916.

The No. 1 Panoram Kodak camera 1900, took $2\frac{1}{2}'' \times 7''$ pictures on what is now 120 size roll film, and can still be used today.

The 'Cirkuit' panoramic camera, courtesy of The Kodak Museum.

ing backs for ordinary cameras, and examples of the many varied and ingenious colour processes that were developed, are wonderful items for the collector. A collection based on them could well become of great value and significance in the near future.

Panoramic cameras, in which the lens swings round in front of the curved film plane producing a long narrow negative, are another example of the unusual cameras that are prized by collectors. The outstanding panoramic camera for the collector is the Thomas Sutton Panoramic Wet Plate Camera made by Thomas Ross of London in 1861. It was fitted with Suttons patent spherical water lens also made by Ross, and used special curved plates. The three examples that have recently come to light have brought prices of up to £11,550 ($26,565) each. The Al-Vista Panoramic camera, marketed by the Multiscope and Film Company, Burlington, Wis., USA, is one that is a little easier to come by today. It had an angle of view of 175 degrees, giving a negative measuring $4'' \times 12''$. It was sold in England in 1899 by Hinton and Company. By 1903, Hinton and Company were manufacturing a panoramic camera of their own. It featured a rising front and the lens could rotate to take a panoramic picture measuring $4'' \times 12''$ or it could be fixed centrally, when it would take ordinary snapshots measuring $4'' \times 6''$. For 1s. 6d. they would send the prospective buyer a specimen panoramic picture, accompanied by the injunction 'Beware of incapable attempts at imitation'.

The so-called 'imitations' referred to were the Panoram Kodaks. These cameras had an angle of view of 142 degrees, producing $3\frac{1}{2}'' \times 12''$ negatives. They were fitted with f 10 rapid rectilinear lenses and brilliant viewfinders, the Model B, having a single speed shutter, and the Model C, a two speed shutter. Kodak introduced the No. 1

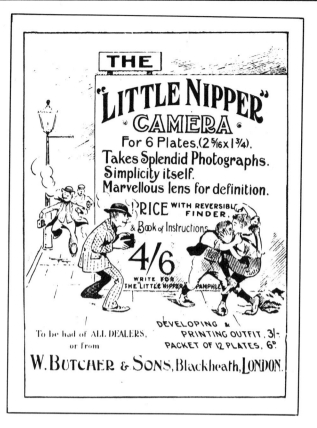

THE "LITTLE NIPPER" CAMERA.
For 6 Plates.(2 5/16 x 1 3/4).
Takes Splendid Photographs.
Simplicity itself.
Marvellous lens for definition.
PRICE WITH REVERSIBLE FINDER.
& Book of Instructions
4/6
WRITE FOR THE LITTLE NIPPER PAMPHLET.
To be had of ALL DEALERS, or from
DEVELOPING & PRINTING OUTFIT, 3/-
PACKET OF 12 PLATES, 6ᴰ.
W. BUTCHER & SONS, Blackheath, LONDON.

Advertisement for W. Butcher and Sons' 'Little Nipper' box camera, 1900.

Panoram Kodak in Great Britain in 1900. This smaller model had an angle of view of 112 degrees, and its negatives measured $2\frac{1}{4}'' \times 7''$.

At the same time as the Kodak saga was unfolding, great numbers of other camera manufacturers were helping to produce the millions of cameras which the rapidly expanding photographic industry demanded. The *British Journal Photographic Almanac* for 1901 contains 519 pages of text—a considerable part of which is concerned with new cameras and apparatus—and no less than 1033 pages of advertisements. This will give some idea of the enormous numbers of cameras and associated items of photographic equipment that were available at the time, and perhaps some idea of the scope that is available to the collector.

Cameras, ranging from the simple box form type, such as the Kodak Brownie and

Newman and Guardia's Universal camera Model 'B' 1895. This camera, No. 181 is a very early example.

(Left) Newman and Guardia's 'Sybyl de Luxe' was still being made and sold in the 1950's.

The London Stereoscopic Company's 'Roylex' camera was made for them by Newman and Guardia.

*Goerz Tropical Tenax ,
1920. The tan leather
bellows match the mahogany
wood, and the dark slides have
polished brass covers.*

*The Voigtlander Vag was a
typical 'folder'.*

the Little Nipper made by W. Butcher and Sons, both designed in 1900 specifically for children, right through a large range of magazine and hand or stand cameras, to the more sophisticated models such as the Adams de Luxe first manufactured in 1899; cameras with double or triple extension, rising and central swing fronts, and revolving backs, whole-plate and larger cameras on massive studio stands, tiny sub-miniatures, and a host of other marvels are all just waiting to be found by the dedicated collector.

The favourite camera of many ordinary amateur photographers in the early years of the twentieth century was the folding hand or pocket camera. These were made by almost every manufacturer, and usually used plates or cut film in single metal slides.

They can be found in large numbers and the simpler versions can still be picked up for £2 ($5) or £3 ($7.50) each. Newman and Guardia's Sibyl was one of the better examples of these metal folding cameras. First marketed in 1906, it was still being sold in the 1950s.

The technically minded collector will appreciate the exceptional qualities of these Sibyl cameras. They were made with a vertical rising front (later ones had a horizontal movement too), a special Newman and Guardia all-metal shutter, and patent lever focusing device. These folding pocket Sibyl cameras were singularly neat and well made, and were indeed a pocket-able camera—the original model measured $5\frac{1}{16}'' \times 3\frac{1}{2}'' \times \frac{13}{16}''$—especially when compared with some of the immense types that had

been called 'pocket' cameras in earlier days. Because of their unique construction, the camera collector would be well advised to try to add some of these Sibyls to his collection. Although large numbers were made during the fifty years or so that they were in production, there was a considerable selection of lenses available, and many modifications were made over the years, including considerable variation in the view-finders that were fitted.

Fallowfield's Central Photographic Stores, of 146 Charing Cross Road, London, who first started in business as photographic manufacturers and dealers in 1856, issued comprehensive catalogues annually from 1862 onwards, each of which is a mine of information for collectors. In their

The Popular Ferrotype camera made by Jonathan Fallowfield 1909 is a good example of a tintype camera.

The American 'Wonder Cannon Automatic Photo-Button Camera' made by the Chicago Ferrotype Co., 1908.

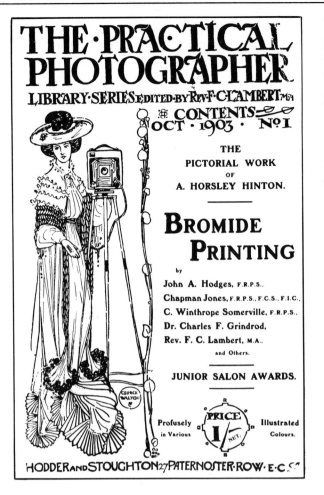

Tropical Heag Model 11/11. Made of impregnated teak with matching light tan 'ant-proof' leather bellows, and lacquered brass fittings, it has an $f4·5$ Eurynar lens in a compur shutter with speeds to 1/200 second.

Most of the leading manufacturers made these lovely tropical versions of their cameras, and the shining wood and gleaming brass makes them wonderfully attractive. So attractive in fact—and so fashionable at the moment—that occasionally I have had to compete with interior decorators when buying them. Wood and brass cameras on a spidery tripod are, I am assured, just the thing to have in the corner of a modern room!

Large numbers of less expensive folding cameras were of course made both before and after World War I, and, being more readily available, will probably become the nucleus of any collection of this type. Typical examples are cameras such as the folding Ensign Klyto, Butcher's Cameo and Klimax, and the Zodel, which were all made in a large range of sizes and models.

Folding cameras will always have a treasured place in the hearts of collectors. Variations of many of them were being sold right up to the end of the 1950s but by 1960 they were obsolete and were no longer manufactured (an exception being the Chinese versions which have recently been imported into England), and have been superseded by the modern single lens reflex and the newer versions of the Instamatic and Polaroid cameras.

Collectors and photographers alike—and many of us are both—have always been fascinated by instant photographs and the various means of making them. To most collectors however the phrase 'instant photographs' calls to mind the pictures of the itinerant street photographer with his tintype portraits. American collectors will find

1913 issue they list no fewer than twenty-one different models of the Sibyl camera.

Another outstanding camera of the folding pocket type, was the Adams Vesta. This was advertised, with no false modesty, as 'the most perfect folding pocket camera made'. One in my collection (serial number 626) is the de luxe model fitted with an $f4·5$ tessar lens in a dial set compur shutter with speeds to 1/200 second, and taking $3\frac{1}{4}'' \times 4\frac{1}{4}''$ plates or film pack adapter. It is something of a rarity as during, and for some years after, World War I the Vesta cameras were only supplied with British made lenses. (This applies of course to most British cameras of this period.) By 1919 some fifteen models of the Vesta were on sale.

One of the outstanding folding cameras in my collection is a 9×12 cm Ernemann

it easier to acquire examples of tintype photographs, as they were sold successfully in the United States from the late 1850s, while in England and Europe they did not become popular until some twenty years later. By the end of the nineteenth century and through the early years of the twentieth however, no fairground, market place or seaside resort in England was complete without a photographer taking instant American tintype portraits.

When tintypes were first introduced ordinary wet plate cameras were used to take them, but cameras were soon being made especially for them and collectors will relish the many weird and wonderful designs that were introduced.

The Telephot Button camera made by the British Ferrotype Company, Blackpool, in 1885 is a fine example of these. One was sold at Christie's sale rooms on Thursday, 4th October 1973 for £252 ($630) which shows their rarity and value today. The lens in those early Button cameras was at the larger end. In later versions the lens was positioned in the smaller end making them look like a cannon.

The American Wonder Cannon Automatic Photo-Button camera of 1908 was one of these later versions and was a great favourite amongst street photographers. The Chicago Ferrotype Company sold this camera for their showrooms in the Chicago Buildings, Whitechapel, Liverpool. Made of nickel-plated copper and aluminium, the Wonder Cannon weighed four pounds. It was one of the quickest ferrotype cameras to use, the manufacturers claiming that it could take and finish the button photographs at a rate of more than six a minute. The Wonder Cannon with its cannon-shaped barrel is a fine example of the out of the ordinary cameras that are such an asset to a collection and so much sought after by collectors.

Ferrotype photographs are still being made in a few places today, but the process lost ground in the 1930s to street photographers who used miniature cameras and these days the 35 mm cameras almost have the beaches and streets to themselves.

Collectors should always look out for items with stories attached to them. Not only individual cameras with special histories, or sets of one manufacturer's cameras, but also sets of cameras that illustrate the development of a process or idea. A showcase exhibiting a progression of these instant cameras, from the early tintype to the Polaroid, together with examples of the images that they created, and perhaps accompanied by manuals or ephemera of the period, is the type of collection to aim for.

It is a lucky collector indeed who is far-sighted enough to foresee the popularity of any one make of camera or photographic speciality. But the current flood of interest in early photographica, together with the gradual drying up of the traditional sources —the antique shop, the junk man and the second-hand camera shop—makes it necessary for both new and established collectors to hunt further afield than was necessary when I began collecting twenty years ago.

The Ermanox was also known as the Ernox f2 focal plane camera when it was introduced into Great Britain in 1925.

CANDID CAMERAS

THE 1920s were a wonderful period for collectable cameras. The improvements made in lenses and sensitized materials during the early part of the twentieth century had led to a new concept in cameras. They began to be designed to use available light, and after World War I several small-plate cameras with extra large lenses were produced. Perhaps the best known of these and the one that all collectors should look for, was the Ermanox focal plane camera. This camera, which used $4 \cdot 5 \times 6$ cm ($1\frac{3}{4}'' \times 2\frac{1}{4}''$) plates, was made at the Ernemann works in Dresden, Germany, in 1924. It was fitted with their new Ernostar $f2$ anastigmat lens and was advertised 'for night photography without flash'.

The Ermanox was a real innovation. The enormous $4''$ $f2$ lens was fitted to a miniature body containing a focal plane shutter. It was a solid well-made little instrument weighing some $3\frac{1}{2}$ lb. The large lens focused from $5'$ to infinity, and it had a folding direct vision viewfinder fitted to the top of the black body.

Dr Eric Salomon, a news reporter of Berlin, became the leading exponent of the 'candid camera', as it was called, taking outstanding photographs of the famous and infamous people of the day with his Ermanox which, because of its huge lens, allowed him to take pictures in lighting conditions that others found impossible. Other photographers followed his example and the Ermanox became extremely successful, both photographically and commercially. But the true future of the candid camera lay in a different direction.

The growth of the cinema industry, and its great commercial success, brought constant improvement to the 35 mm film that had become the standard size. Mass production of this film to meet the ever growing demands of the film studios meant that it was readily available, and many miniature still cameras were soon being designed to use it. These early 35 mm cameras are of great significance to the collector and photographic historian, and are a real landmark on the road to modern photography.

The first 35 mm still camera to be produced commercially was the Homeos stereoscopic camera manufactured by Richard Frères in Paris. The Homeos was patented in 1913 and the first 150 were made by the end of that year. It took a pair of 18×24 mm frames (there is a two-frame space between the stereo pair) and the film advances two frames at a time.

The Homeos is one of the really rare 35 mm cameras. World War I interrupted its manufacture and only some 1,500 had been made when production was stopped in

(Left), The Homeos stereoscopic camera was the first commercially produced camera using 35 mm cine film for still photography. 150 were manufactured by the end of 1913.

(Right) The Ansco Memo, one of the earliest 'half-frame' 35mm cameras.

Advertisement for the Tourist Multiple camera and projector, from The Photographic Dealer for March 1914.

TOURIST MULTIPLE CAMERA AND PROJECTION LANTERN

These Two Form a Unit Equipment Entirely Novel in Idea and Almost Automatic in Action, Combining All the Perfection and Convenience of Motion Pic-ture Photography Without its Excessive Expense.

750 Individual Exposures Without Reloading with a Camera Only 4x8x2½ Inches in Size

The most perfect, compact and complete camera ever invented. Every traveler, lecturer, explorer, camper, is a prospective buyer. Its appeal is immediate to everyone who wishes to take a large number of pictures for future illustrative purposes with the minimum of trouble and expense, and the maximum of convenience and certainty. Enlargements of almost any size can be made without loss of sharpness, or without cutting or injuring the strip negative.

The camera carries 50 feet of standard, perforated motion picture film in a reloadable magazine, with a capacity of 750 pictures without reloading. You can take snapshots as simply and quickly as pulling the trigger of a repeating rifle.

It is very compact, being but 4x8x2⅜ inches in size, and has a special anastigmatic lens of microscopic sharpness and great rapidity, working at F.2.5.

It is beautifully finished, made of aluminum and so constructed as to be practically heat, cold and damp-proof. This insures the preservation of the film, whether in the Tropics or the Arctic regions, and the whole matter of developing and printing can safely be left until the return home.

It is easy to carry, always ready and exceedingly simple to operate both for oblong or upright pictures.

Everyone interested in photography, amateur or professional, can use one and will want one.

All the Pictures Thrown on a Screen in the Order They Were Taken, by a Touch of the Finger!

A complete diary of everything interesting and exciting on a whole trip or tour simply and graphically shown in clear, well-defined pictures.

This Projection Lantern is of entirely new and advanced design. It is very compactly constructed and fitted with a high-grade projection lens especially adapted for the work.

A positive film, made from the strip negative at very slight expense, is used; and it is far superior to ordinary lantern slides.

Compare the space taken up by 750 glass lantern slides to that occupied by the same number of pictures on a roll of film you can nearly hide in your hand!

Besides, the film positive is unbreakable; the change to the next picture is automatic, and the presentation of the pictures in the wrong sequence is impossible.

The lantern is complete with arc lamp, rheostat, wires, etc., and is readily attached to any 110 volt circuit by means of a plug.

Its manipulation is simple, its pictures perfect, and its opportunities for use in business, in the home, for professional and educational purposes, is unlimited.

The instant appeal of this latest and greatest achievement in photography is so great that it will create an immediate demand.

Fully illustrated book containing all particulars will be sent on request.

HERBERT & HUESGEN COMPANY　　　**456 FOURTH AVENUE, NEW YORK, U.S.A.**

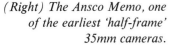

the early 1920s, supposedly because of the difficulty of obtaining supplies of the 35 mm film in the appropriate wrapping. However, they were shown in dealers' catalogues until all the stocks were finally cleared in the early 1930s.

An even earlier 35 mm still camera had been developed in 1912 by George P. Smith of Missouri, USA. Designed to produce the now standard size 24 × 36 cm negatives, it was never put into large scale production. The Simplex Multi-Exposure camera, manufactured by the Multi-Speed Shutter Company, was another American 35 mm camera. Made in 1914, it used 50′ rolls of standard perforated motion picture film to produce either 800 half-frame or 400 whole-frame pictures.

Another, and perhaps more successful 35 mm camera, was the Tourist Multiple camera, made by the Herbert and Huesgen Company of 456, Fourth Avenue, New York, in 1914. Using standard 35 mm cine film in a reloadable magazine, it took 750 half-frame (18 × 24 cm) pictures on each load of film. The negative film strip could be used to produce individual prints, which could be considerably enlarged, or it could be used to produce a positive film strip for projection, and a special projection lantern using an electric arc lamp was produced by the manufacturers for this purpose. In their book *Glass, Brass and Chrome, The American 35 mm camera*, published by the University of Oklahoma Press, the authors, Kalton C. Lahue and Joseph A. Bailey, give a production figure of only 1,000 for this camera, and it is correspondingly rare today. Originally sold for £50 ($125) I would hesitate to guess what sort of price one would fetch today, but it would take a wealthy collector indeed to top the bidding for one at an auction.

It was in 1914, too, that James H. Sinclair of the Haymarket, London, produced the Centus film camera. This was a box camera which took spools of standard 35 mm cine film, an additional special perforation being used to space the frames. Each spool carried sufficient film for 100 exposures. The Levy-Roth Minnigraph, which was sold in Berlin in 1914, was another pre-World War I camera that used standard 35 mm cine film, taking fifty frames, 18 × 24 mm, on each load. The war stopped the production of all of these early 35 mm cameras, and they were not reintroduced afterwards as was the Homeos. Estimated production figures varying from a few hundred to about a thousand of each model are probably accurate and very few examples are extant.

The first successful easy loading 35 mm camera was undoubtedly the 1924 Ansco Memo. All one had to do with this little American gem was to thread the end of the film into the take-up cartridge, and the camera carried on from there. Up to fifty exposures could be taken on each easy load film cartridge.

Collectors will find associated with this Ansco Memo camera one of the early systems of accessories. There was a special developing apparatus, a film strip printer, a film strip projector, and a fitted focus enlarging printer. Ansco also produced several different folding models of this camera during the 1930s, and these they called the Memar cameras.

Shortly after paying £5 ($12.50) for an early Ansco Memo in 1971 (early ones can be recognized by their wooden film boxes, later examples had metal ones), I saw a Boy Scout Memo, described as 'the olive drab paint does have minor chips. Two screws missing from finder' priced at £36 ($90) in an American catalogue. Although prices in the United States are usually rather higher than in Great Britain, I thought this was unrealistically high for a native American camera that originally cost $20 and was made in considerable

quantities for many years.

However, the candid cameras that outsold all the others, and those that all collectors look for today, are the early models of the Leica. The first six Leicas were made in 1923, production continued in 1924, and they were introduced to the public at the 1925 Leipzig Fair in Germany. They soon became the international symbol of photographic excellence. Noted for their high grade workmanship, quality, and durability, original Model I Leicas made forty-five years ago are still in use and producing first class photographs today.

The metal parts of the first Leica model were enamelled black (later versions were also made with nickel-plated metal parts) and it had an $f3.5$ non-interchangeable 50 mm Elmar lens that had been especially designed for it by Dr Max Berek. It was a staggering success and its wonderful quality set the standard for a whole new generation of cameras.

Of especial interest to collectors are the very few early Leica Is which were fitted with an even earlier lens, the Elmax (which was also designed by Dr Berek), and which are extremely rare and valuable today. When looking for these early models of the Leica it should be remembered that the Leica serial numbers started with No. 100, and not with No. 1.

Another great rarity for the collector is the Compur Leica. Instead of the focal plane shutter, the Elmar lenses of these models were fitted in a compur shutter with speeds from 1 to 1/300 seconds. Two different types of Compur Leicas were made. In the earlier ones, manufactured from 1926 until 1929, the shutter was of the dial set type. The shutters of the later Compur Leicas were of the rim set type (instead of having a small separate dial on the front of the camera, the shutter was set by a knurled rim fitted around the front of the lens) and these were made in 1929 and 1930.

These are the official Compur Leica production lists:

Serial numbers	Total	Dates	Type
5,700 to 6,300	600	'1926 to 1929	Dial set
13,100 to 13,300	200	1929	Rim set
21,479 to 21,810	331	1930	Rim set
34,451 to 34,802	351	1930	Rim set

Because of World War II and other events beyond the control of the manufacturers, these official listings, showing a total production of 1,482 Compur Leicas (out of a total of over a million Leicas built to date) are not strictly accurate. I know of rim set Compur Leicas with serial numbers 32,731 and 32,732, and several with numbers over 40,000 are known, so it is safe to assume that at least two other batches were made. Any collector would relish an example of the De Luxe Leica I that was pro-

An original prototype of the Leica. The speeds were changed by varying the tension of the fixed slit non-capping shutter. Un-named when it was made in 1912-13, it was later refered to as the UR-Leica. Courtesy of E. J. Newton, President of the Leica Historical Society.

A very early Leica camera No. 113. Courtesy of George Gordon Carr.

The dial-set version of the Compur Leica. courtesy of Hans Edwards.

duced in 1930. Covered with brown lizard skin and with gold-plated metal parts, they were advertised 'for the use of ladies and Maharajas'. The only one that I know of in private hands is in the collection of Michel Auer in Switzerland.

During that same year Leitz introduced a new Model I with interchangeable lenses. These lenses and bodies were, however, not standardized and the lenses often had to be especially adjusted for each different body. From March 1931 (camera No. 60,500) the lens screw mount and the lens flange were strictly standardized, and any Leica lens would fit on to any Leica camera.

The Standard Leica, with numbers from 100,000 onwards, was introduced in 1932. This was made in either black or chromium finish, and can easily be distinguished from the earlier Leica I by its narrower, extending film rewinding knob.

The Leica II, which was also available from 1932, was the first to be made with a built-in coupled rangefinder. Available in either the black enamelled or chromium finishes, its serial numbers ran from 71,500 onwards. The Leica III was produced in 1933, as an improvement on the Leica II. The Model II had a focal plane shutter with speeds of 1/20 to 1/500, second and time, whilst the Model III had in addition a slow-speed dial on the front of the camera with settings from 1 to 1/20 second, and a magnifying lens in the rangefinder. The addition of an eyelet at each end for a carrying strap is another simple way of identifying this model, the serial numbers of which start at 109,000.

American collectors will know that instead of being numbered the Leica models marketed in the United States were identified by the letters of the alphabet. Thus the

Model I is the American Model A; the Compur Leica, the Model B; the Model I with interchangeable lenses, Model C; the Model II, Model D; and so on.

The Leica IIIa was the same as Model III, but with an additional shutter speed of 1/1,000 second. Produced in 1935, it had serial numbers from 156,201. The Leica IIIb, which was introduced in 1938 with serial numbers running from 240,001, had adjustable magnification in the rangefinder (the lever for this is placed next to the rewind knob), and had the eye pieces of its rangefinder and viewfinder close together.

The collector will be more interested in unusual and rarer models such as the Leica 250 and the Leica 72. The Leica 250 was made in the middle 1930s, although not introduced into Great Britain until 1937. Designed to be used by beach or street photographers or reporters it was basically a model IIIa with extra large cassette spaces which took special cassettes holding ten metres (33') of film. The Leica 72 made in Canada in 1954, was similar to the model IIIa, but took seventy-two half-frame exposures (18 × 24 mm) on a standard thirty-six exposure film. This is the only half-frame Leica, and very few were made. (Their serial numbers were from 357,301 to 357,500.) The 72 will soon be classed as one of the most rare Leicas of all, and would be of outstanding interest in any collection. I have not seen a Leica 72 offered for sale recently, but examples of the Leica 250, which change hands in England for about £200 each these days, sell for £400 ($1,000) in the United States.

Another unusual camera made by Leica was the single exposure Leica that was available from 1930 and designed for testing lenses and films. It had a black lacquered tube-like body which could be fitted with any Leica lens. The rear of the camera could take a ground glass screen or a single dark slide holding a 40 mm length of 35 mm

The rim-set version of the Compur Leica.

The Leica instruction booklet of 1928, now reprinted for collectors by Morgan and Morgan Inc., New York.

film. It was supplied with an Ibsor diaphragm shutter, but I have also seen one fitted with a dial-set compur shutter. In America, early in 1973, it was claimed that Leica cameras retained their value to such an extent that many of their old cameras were worth as much or more second-hand as they had cost when new, and they quoted the following prices for used cameras in good condition to justify this claim. The Model A

The Leica 72 manufactured by Ernst Leitz of Canada is one of the more rare examples of the Leica camera. Courtesy of Hans Edwards.

It is estimated that only twenty-four of these gilt finished snakeskin covered Luxus Leicas were made. One batch was made in 1930 with serial Nos. 34803-34817 and a couple with slightly later numbers have also been located. Courtesy of Hans Edwards.

This Leica 250 has been completely overhauled and re-built by George Gordon Carr, and is now a wonderful collector's item. Courtesy of Hans Edwards.

The Luftwaffe Leica, a 10.5cm Mountain Elmar lens, a 5cm f1.5 Xenon (nickel finish), and the Leica single exposure device with slide are all scarce collector's items from Leitz. Courtesy of Hans Edwards.

that cost £20.25 ($81) when new in 1929 now sells for £80 ($200). Model B (the rare Compur Leica) that originally cost £23.75 ($95), now fetches about £400 ($1,000) and a Model D which cost £25 ($100) new in 1935 now costs £50 ($125). Even second-hand examples of comparatively modern models such as the 1958 IIIG, the 1960 M3, and the 1969 M4, in nice condition, sell for about the same prices today as when they were first made, and this is just one more reason for the great popularity of the Leica with camera collectors.

Thematic camera collections, that is those devoted to one particular subject or theme, are among the most interesting of all, and outstanding collections have been based on the many imitations of the Leica that have been made by different manufacturers. Collectable copies of the Leicas have been made in almost every camera producing country in the world, and these copy Leicas run the whole range from cheap imitations to outright forgeries. (A few of the early Fed cameras made in Russia were actually engraved with the Leitz 'Leica' trade mark.)

Aside from the Russian Fed, collectors can search for examples of Leica imitations like the American Kardon, the several versions of the British Reid, and Japanese cameras such as the early rangefinder Canon, the Leotax, and the Nicca cameras, to make the basis of a collection of this type.

The Leica was perhaps the most revolutionary camera since George Eastman's Kodak. Many other 35 mm cameras were made, but its first real competitor, and the next important camera for the collector, was the Zeiss Ikon Contax.

The Contax I was manufactured for four years, from early in 1932 until late in 1936, but was still listed by the manufacturers until the end of 1937. Two distinct varieties were made. The original Contax had shutter speeds from 1/25 to 1/100 seconds and B., whilst the later one had additional slow speeds from ½ second. It is easily identified by its all-black body with nickel trim, separate eyepieces for the view-finder and rangefinder, and the film winding shutter setting knob on the front. An American collector, Robert A. Helm, writing in the *Graphic Antiquarian* of January 1972 catalogues five versions of this first Contax which were all called the Contax I, but most collectors will be happy with the two easily distinguishable models. The Contax II and Contax III (which was the same camera but with a built on photo-electric exposure meter) were made from 1936 to 1940. Their chrome finish, winding knob on the top instead of the front of the camera, combined viewfinder/rangefinder eyepiece, and speeds from ½ to 1/1250 seconds (the post-war Contax IIA had slow speeds from 1 second) makes them readily recognizable to the collector.

The Leotax with f3.5 Topcor lens.

The Nicca with f2 Niccor lens.

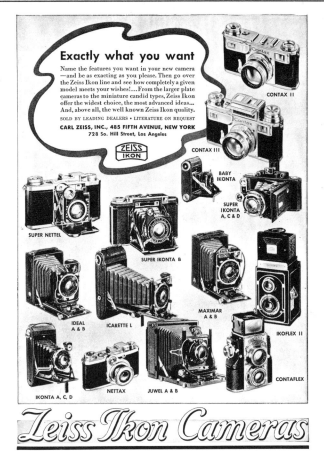

Zeiss Ikon produced many other outstanding cameras during the 1930s that are sought after by collectors. For instance, the Super Nettel a quality 35 mm folding camera with a focal plane shutter with speeds of 1/5 to 1/1000 seconds; the Nettax, which was a cross between the Contax and the Super Nettel; and the Tenax, which took negatives 24 × 24 mm on 35 mm film, are a few examples of the kind of camera the collector should be seeking.

The advertisement reproduced here from the *American Annual of Photography* of 1938 shows just a few of the great variety of models which were then available from Zeiss Ikon who were only one of the large number of manufacturers then producing first class cameras in every industrialized country in the world. This once again shows the vast field that a collection of cameras can encompass, and emphasizes the need for specialization, so that a collection really representative of one section or another can be brought together.

Amongst many other outstanding 35 mm cameras, the collector will find the Kodak Retina of interest. Three variations were made, in 1934, 1935 and 1936, all with black bodies trimmed with nickel. The film advance release on the back, instead of on the top of the camera as in the two earlier models—the film transport had to be unlocked after each exposure—distinguishes the 1936 model, while the Retina I of 1937 had a satin chrome finish. The Retina II, manufactured in 1936, was the first model with a coupled rangefinder. Many more models of this camera were also brought out both before and after World War II.

The Robot I was another of the fascinating collectors' cameras of the 1930s. This little treasure took fifty exposures, 24 × 24 mm (1″ × 1″), on a standard cassette load of 35 mm film. Aptly named the Robot, its novelty lies in the clockwork motor that is built into the body of the camera. The shutter on all the models is a rotary blade behind the lens type which is released in the normal way. When the shutter closes however the motor transports the film, sets the shutter for the next exposure and moves the exposure counter all in a fraction of a second, so rapidly that six or eight exposures per second can be made, and twenty-four exposures can be made with one winding of the spring. It would only accept the special Robot cassettes.

The Robot I was the only model with the slow shutter speed of 1 second—speeds on all the other models start from $\frac{1}{2}$ second—and its exposure counter is only marked from 1 to 24, so that exposure number 25 is shown as number 1 again. Collectors will find that two versions of the Robot I were made, the later model having a shutter release locking ring to prevent accidental exposure.

*The Contax 1.
Manufactured with slight
modifications from 1932 to
1936.*

The Robot II, made from 1938, is easily identified by the single flash contact on the front of the camera. It has a safety catch for the shutter release button, and the fixed viewfinder is fitted with a movable prism. This model was also made with a double spring motor which exposed forty-eight negatives with one winding, instead of the usual twenty-four. The motor winding knob protrudes about $1\frac{1}{2}''$ above the top of this model.

The Robot that collectors hunt for is the rarely seen Luftwaffe Robot. Produced from 1940 to 1945, it was used by the German Air Force as a gun camera in World War II. This camera was a simplified version of the Robot II, fitted with the double spring motor and chrome lens mount, and both the body of the camera and the back of the lens were stamped 'Luftwaffe Eigentum' (Luftwaffe Property). Very few of these cameras have come out of Germany since the war.

By the late 1930s almost every camera manufacturer had jumped on to the candid camera bandwagon, and a multitude of miniature cameras were being produced. Miniatures were cameras taking everything up to and including $2\frac{1}{4}'' \times 2\frac{1}{4}''$ negatives and the 'Special Miniature Camera Number' of the *Amateur Photographer* of 22nd June 1938 listed 132 such cameras—some in as many as sixteen different versions. Many fancy formats were dreamed up, and cameras using these now forgotten film sizes are rich regions for the collector. The Vest Pocket 127 film size, making eight $1\frac{5}{8}'' \times 2\frac{1}{2}''$ exposures, that had been introduced by Kodak together with their Vest Pocket Kodak cameras in 1912, was rapidly adopted by other camera manufacturers. The Ihagee Autolette was a folding 127 roll film camera, and the Ihagee Weeny Ultix introduced in Great Britain in 1932 used 127 film or $1\frac{5}{8}'' \times 2\frac{1}{2}''$ plates in single slides. Sold fitted with

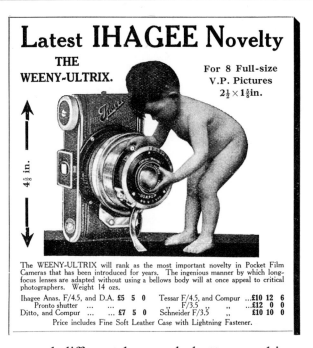

several different lens and shutter combinations, collectors should look for the top models of both these cameras which were fitted with *f* 3·5 tessar lenses in compur shutters. In the 1920s Zeiss Ikon evolved the Kolibri, a small camera taking sixteen 3 × 4 cm exposures on the same size spool. This was to become the new fashion, and many excellent cameras were made which combined compactness and economy.

The Kodak Bantams were another series of simple cameras made at Kodak's Rochester factory. Kodak introduced Bantam cameras and the 828 roll film for them in June 1935. One of our forgotten film sizes, 828 was paper-backed unperforated 35 mm film that gave eight 28 × 40 mm exposures.

Eleven different versions of the Bantam are listed in the *Kodak Collector*, together with the Kodak Pony 828 camera that was made from 1949 to 1959. Although the cameras are now discontinued Kodak still market the 828 film for them. The dream model was the Bantam Special. Two versions of the Specials were made. The first, on sale from 1936 to 1940 was fitted with a 4·5 cm Kodak Ektar *f* 2 lens in a compur rapid shutter, and the second one, marketed from

1941 to 1948, can be recognized by its *f* 2 Kodak Ektar lens in a Supermatic shutter. It is these two, together with the Bantams that were used by the Royal Air Force during World War II, that are the outstanding collectable models.

Simple cameras such as the Six-20 Jiffy Kodak of 1933 and the Series II model of 1937 were made in large numbers. Both of these models have spring-open fronts, an instantaneous and time shutter, and a Twindar lens. Attractive little cameras such as these should not be overlooked by the collector. Although unpretentious, they serve to highlight the more outstanding specimens in a collection and contrast pleasantly with more elaborate items.

The folding roll film camera which was once so popular is practically non-existent today but many of these fabulous folders can still be found, and a collection could be built up with little effort. The Krauss-Peggy, made in 1933, was one of the fine folders of its day. Despite weighing nearly 1½ lb—heavier than a Leica—it only measured 1″ × 5″ × 2″ when closed, against the Leica's 1¼″ × 5⅜″ × 2¼″, and the special compur shutter which was fitted had speeds ranging from 1 to 1/300 seconds. Some other typical examples of the folding roll film camera would be a selection of the many versions of the Zeiss Ikon Ikonta. These lovely all-metal cameras were made in several sizes. They opened at the touch of a button, the bellows extending and the direct vision viewfinder springing up almost with lives of their own. The New Ikonta (model 520) was a typical example. First made in 1932 an improved version is dated 1933 because its *f* 4·5 Nover-Anastigmat lens in a compur shutter was first introduced in that year.

Other improved versions of this camera were the Super Ikontas of 1934 which featured a coupled distance meter, and were again made in several sizes, and the Super Ikonta No. 530/16 of 1935 which took eleven

The first Kodak Retina was introduced in 1934. This is a later version which has the black stove enamel of the very first Retina but has the film release and reversing lever on the back of the camera instead of the top. After 1936 this Retina (which was called the Retina I when the Retina II with coupled rangefinder was introduced in 1937), had chrome finished metal parts.

pictures on the usual $2\frac{1}{4}'' \times 3\frac{1}{4}''$ roll film spool. This is easily recognized as it had the baseplate hinged in the centre of one of its longer sides, and so had a horizontal look rather than the vertical look of the earlier models.

All camera collectors are interested in history, and the name of Voigtländer has been associated with the history of photography from its earliest days. During the 1930s, the Voigtländer factory produced many first-class collectable cameras. One such was the Bessa. Introduced in 1933 it was fitted with either a Skopar f 4·5, or Heliar f 4·5 lens in a compur shutter. The Rangefinder Bessa was another Voigtländer winner. The 1937 model featured a coupled rangefinder, hinged filter, and a trigger shutter release built in to the base board. With an f 3·5 lens in a compur rapid shutter, it was a camera to be proud of.

Houghton-Butcher Limited of London

Left:– Postage stamp camera by W. Butcher 1908 sold for £367 ($845) Right:– Eureka camera made by W. W. Rouch 1895 with two shutters, one behind the lens and the other a focal plane, sold for £399 ($918). These cameras were sold at Christies on 25th April 1974. The sliding box camera was not included in this sale. Courtesy of Christies.

are another firm that was involved in the history of photography from the beginning, and it would probably be impossible to make a complete list of their collectors' pieces. George Houghton became a partner in Antoine Claudet's glass business in 1836 and Claudet and Houghton became the only importers of daguerreotype cameras and equipment, and of daguerreotypes, and their history is of great importance to the camera collector. The daguerreotypes that they imported—mainly views of Paris, Rome and other continental cities—were sold at prices ranging from one guinea to four guineas or more, depending on their size, quality and interest. By July 1840 they were also advertising daguerreotypes of London, probably taken by Claudet himself.

Early street scenes of this nature are extremely rare and valuable today, and are highly prized by collectors. At the collectors' sale at Sotheby's on Wednesday, 13th December 1972, 'Two Rare and Early Daguerreotypes', a view of Rouen Cathedral and a view of Parliament Street, London, both measuring $5\frac{1}{2}'' \times 4''$, attributed to M.de St Croix, were sold for £450 ($1,125). A group of three similar ones, another view of Rouen Cathedral, and views of St

Martin-in-the-Fields' clock tower and the National Gallery, brought in £460 ($1,150). If any of Claude's daguerreotypes of London views come to light they would probably fetch prices of a similar nature.

Over the years the business was built up by absorbing many smaller firms, culminating in the amalgamation with W. Butcher and Sons Limited on 1st January 1926. In the 304 page catalogue which Houghton-Butcher Limited issued then, they listed 534 lens, shutter, and size permutations of the forty-six different cameras that they were making, as well as a multitude of accessories. By the 1930s they were proudly claiming that their Ensign camera works at Walthamstow, London, was the 'largest camera factory in the British Empire!' and were turning out candid cameras by the cartload.

The Purma Special, a simple candid camera that was first marketed in 1937, is also of interest because of its novel method of controlling the speed of its metal focal plane shutter. When held horizontally in the normal way the shutter speed was 1/150 second. If the camera was held in a vertical position with the shutter release button on the right the shutter speed became 1/25

Cover of W. Butcher and Sons
Ltd. catalogue 1910.

Left:– The Ensign Cupid
roll film camera 1922.
Right:– The original prototype
patented by V. W. Edwards in
1921 from which the Ensign-
Cupid was developed.

Giant model of an Ensign
folding camera entered by the
Houghton-Butcher Mfg. Co.
Ltd. in the Walthamstow
Carnival at London E.17 in the
1920's.

second, and when it was held vertically with the shutter release on the left the speed became 1/450 second. A pivoted brass weight altered the width of the slit in the focal plane shutter according to the camera position, from approximately $\frac{1}{16}''$ to $\frac{1}{2}''$. This weight also altered the shutter speed, by either pulling with the spring for the high speed or against it for the low. The shutter could not be released without first removing the lens cap, which caused the lens to spring out into position. Moulded out of bakelite, the Purma Special measured $2\frac{1}{4}'' \times 6'' \times 2\frac{3}{4}''$ and weighed 12 oz.

Many of the post-war 35 mm cameras are collectable too, especially if they are as outstanding as the Bell and Howell Foton 35 mm sequence camera introduced in 1948; or as novel as the 35 mm still cameras with triple lens turrets, of which the Rectaflex Rotor is a typical example; or as lovely as the Casca, which was one of the first new cameras to be produced in Germany after World War II.

By concentrating on candid cameras, a collection can be built up fairly easily. Inexpensive examples of many of the cameras that were made during the twenty-one years between the two World Wars can still be found in second-hand camera shops.

Collectors will find a fund of information about candid cameras in the photographic magazines of the period. The English *Amateur Photographer*, the American *Modern Photography*, and *Popular Photography*, amongst others, listed all the cameras that were available at the time. Many post-war magazines have carried references and reports too. The annual *Photography Directory* and *Buying Guides* compiled by the editors of *Popular Photography* contained 'Prices—descriptions—illustrations of virtually every piece of photographic equipment' of the day, whilst the *Camera Buying Guides* published annually in the December issues of *Modern Photography* since 1956 give details of hundreds of new and used cameras.

*The Kombi, 'a combined camera
and graphascope', advertisement
1895.*

SUB-MINIATURE CAMERAS

ALL collectors are magpies, and camera collectors are no exception to this. We will not willingly pass, or part with, anything of photographic interest. Sooner or later, we all run out of space in which to keep our collections and one of the obvious answers to this problem is to collect smaller or sub-miniature cameras. Small cameras are always interesting, the smallest are almost like jewellery. These little gems are so attractive that they have often been collected by people who are not interested in photography or cameras, and so have been preserved where larger cameras would have been discarded or destroyed. These days 'sub-miniature' means a camera using a 16 mm or smaller film but in my collection I class all cameras that were extra small, compared with the usual size of cameras in their day, as sub-miniature.

Small cameras have been made and used since the beginning of photography. The earliest sub-miniature was made by Niépce. His first camera made in 1816 was a home-made 6″ wooden box. When he broke the lens of this camera, he made a second one using a little jewel box that measured about 3.5×4 cm which he fitted with a microscope lens. This was surely the world's first sub-miniature camera.

Daguerre worked with larger cameras but Fox Talbot used cameras so small that his wife referred to them as his 'mouse-traps'. Many of his early paper negatives measured no more than $1″ \times 1″$, and his cameras were correspondingly minute.

The first successful photographic portraits were taken with a reflecting camera invented by the American Alexander Wolcott in October 1839. In March the

following year Wolcott and his partner, John Johnson, opened the world's first portrait studio, their famous Daguerrean Parlour, in New York City. Instead of a lens the front of the Wolcott camera was open, and the image was reflected from a concave metal mirror at the rear of the camera back onto the sensitized plate.

Production models of this camera measured $8'' \times 8\frac{1}{2}'' \times 15''$ and produced a miniature daguerreotype measuring $1\frac{3}{4}'' \times 2\frac{1}{4}''$. The $7''$ metal mirror which was used in this camera concentrated much more light onto the plate than was possible with any of the other types of camera then in use. It was this which allowed them to make satisfactory exposures in as little as 4 or 5 minutes, as against the 20 or 30 minutes that had previously been necessary. These cameras were sold successfully in the United States and in England.

Improvements in the daguerreotype process itself, and new faster lenses, soon made larger cameras popular, and it is these large ones that are usually seen in museums and collections. But throughout the formative years of photography the need for small-sized cameras was felt.

Charles Piazzi Smyth, the Astronomer Royal for Scotland and the author of the first book to be illustrated with real stereoscopic photographs (*Teneriffe an Astronomer's Experiment*, published in 1858), took a miniature camera of his own design with him when he went to Egypt in 1865 to study the pyramids. It used the standard $1'' \times 3''$ microscope slides for plates, sensitizing the bottom inch to produce a negative $1''$ square. The sensitizing and subsequent development of the plate was done inside the body of the camera. Piazzi Smyth was the first to suggest

Alexander S. Wolcott's prototype reflecting daguerreotype camera 1840, measured $2'' \times 2'' \times 4''$ and used $\frac{3}{8}''$ square plates.

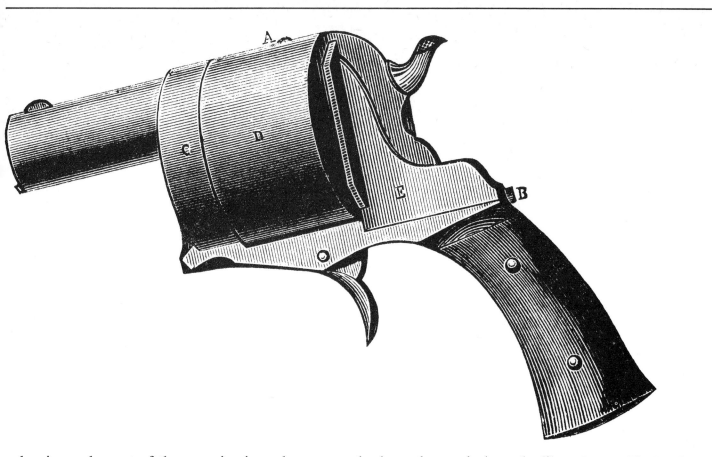

The French photo revolver 1886 is one of those legendary cameras that any collector would love to find.

enlarging only part of the negative in order to produce a cropped picture. Cameras of this kind are few and far between but it is this rarity as much as any technical innovation they may embody that makes them so desirable to the collector today. Early cameras of any kind are extremely hard to find now, and should be treasured by any collector who is lucky enough to locate one.

The pleasure of finding and preserving these fine examples of early cameras is greatly increased when they are unusual. One such out-of-the-ordinary miniature dry plate camera in my collection, made by Marion and Company of London in 1884, took photographs $1\frac{1}{4}''$ square on gelatine dry plates. I am still grateful to the friendly antique dealer who spotted it in a country shop, and bought it for me. The speed of these gelatine plates made a shutter necessary, and this camera is fitted with a simple drop-type shutter. It worked well

enough, but obscured the tube-like view-finder on the top of the camera when the exposure was made. I paid £10 for it, and this again illustrates the wide variance in camera prices today. Examples of miniature cameras made a little later than this have recently brought much higher prices at Christie's. An early all-metal dry plate camera of 1890 was sold for £180 ($450) on Thursday, 14th December 1972, and another, this time without the gravity shutter brought £450 ($1,080) at Sotheby's on 21st March, 1975.

The Kombi camera is another interesting 'little bit different' model of the type that is an asset to any collection, for when the back was removed it became a viewer. Its name was derived from the legend 'A Combined Camera and Graphoscope', which is engraved on the front of the camera. Patented in the USA by the inventor W.V. Esmond of Chicago, Illinois, in December 1892, patents were applied for

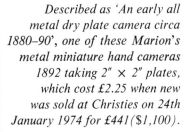

Sub-miniature camera by Marion and Co. of London taking $1\frac{1}{4}'' \times 1\frac{1}{4}''$ plates, 1884.

Described as 'An early all metal dry plate camera circa 1880–90', one of these Marion's metal miniature hand cameras 1892 taking $2'' \times 2''$ plates, which cost £2.25 when new was sold at Christies on 24th January 1974 for £441($1,100).

in the entire world. A.C. Kemper became his partner and created the Kombi Camera Company. Kombi cameras were first marketed in 1893 and during the next four years large numbers were manufactured. Kemper claimed that he sold 50,000 in one year and one sub-contractor, the Scovill and Adams Company, produced some 110,000 Kombis for him. Modifications were made from time to time and a patent for an improved version of the Kombi was granted in February 1895. The Kombi measured $1\frac{5}{8}'' \times 1\frac{5}{8}'' \times 2''$. It was made of oxidized metal and took photographs either $1\frac{1}{8}''$ square or, using the wooden mask supplied with the camera, round ones $1\frac{1}{8}''$ in diameter.

I paid £3 ($7.50) each for both of my Kombi cameras, the first about six years ago and the second about three years ago,

but of course they fetch much higher prices than that today.

At a time when most men wore pocket watches this was an obvious shape for a small camera, and several manufacturers made cameras of this type. With a little luck the collector will be able to find one of the Lancaster Patent Watch cameras which were made in 1891. This little beauty sprang open at a touch and took photographs measuring $2'' \times 1\frac{1}{2}''$ using single-plate holders. It was made by J. Lancaster and Son, of Birmingham, England.

The Ticka watch camera, made by Houghtons Limited of London, was perhaps the earliest cassette loading sub-miniature. This was the English version of the Expo watch camera manufactured by the Expo Camera Company of New York.

The Ticka watch camera, 'Every tick a picture', had a fixed focus 30 mm f 16 meniscus lens and its short focal length ensured that everything from about 3′ to infinity was in focus. The lens was in the winding stem of the watch, and the winding knob was a lens cap which had to be removed before making each exposure, and replaced whilst setting the shutter.

In 1908 two new versions of the Ticka were introduced. The Focal Plane Ticka and the Watch Face Ticka which had a glass-covered enamelled watch dial on the back instead of the monogram. The watch hands were fixed at seven minutes past ten, and indicated the angle covered by the lens, making it easier to take photographs with the camera concealed in the hand, instead of using the viewfinder.

Several small alterations were made to both the Ticka and the Expo cameras, which were identical in appearance except for the name on the case, during the time that they were manufactured, and several different viewfinders were marketed. They were sold successfully right up to 1914.

(Above) Kombi sub-miniature camera 1893.

(Far left) Three miniature cameras sold at Christies on 14th June 1973.
Left:– Marion metal miniature camera 1884 sold for £252 ($630).
Centre:– Marion Academy camera 1883 £651 ($1625).
Right:– An early metal dry plate camera 1880-90 (without the drop shutter) £378 ($945).
Courtesy of Christies.

Academy camera by Marion and Co. The magazine holds twelve $1\frac{1}{4}'' \times 1\frac{1}{4}''$ plates.

Magic Photoret pocket watch camera, 1890. Courtesy of The Kodak Museum.

The Expo Camera Company also made the Expo Police camera which they patented in 1911. This all-metal camera measured $2\frac{1}{2}'' \times 3\frac{3}{8}'' \times 1''$ and had a fixed focus achromatic lens with a choice of two stops.

Collectors should aim for complete sets of Ticka and Expo cameras and their accessories. Many collectable cameras were made in such a large variety of models that it would be almost impossible to make a definitive collection of them. Cameras such as the Ticka and Expo, however, of which only a small number of models and variations were made for a comparatively few years, permit the collector to put together a comprehensive collection. A complete collection of this kind attains an importance and value far in excess of that of its individual parts, and is one of the contributions that the serious collector can make to the history of photography.

The Demon Detective camera, made in 1893 by the American Camera Company, and the Presto Pocket camera, made in 1899 by E.B. Koopman of New York, are excellent American examples of some of the unusual cameras that were made at the end of the last century.

In 1905 Thornton Pickard made the Snappa, a simple camera taking $1\frac{3}{4}'' \times 2\frac{5}{16}''$ plates. The Snappa reverted to the earliest form of camera, being simply two leather covered boxes sliding one inside the other. When the front was drawn out it clicked into position and the camera could be used as a simple focus box camera, but an accessory focusing screen with hood was soon made available and this made the Snappa a more versatile little camera.

The Argus, made in 1909, is another unusual little collectable camera. Looking like a monocular or small telescope it took a photograph on $4 \cdot 5 \times 6$ cm plates at right angles to the direction in which it was pointed. Fitted with a time and instantaneous shutter, it was sold in England by May and Company, of Seacombe, Liverpool. Watson and Sons marketed an improved version of this camera in March 1914, with speeds of 1/25, 1/50 and 1/75 seconds. It is interesting to note that all these speeds could be increased by about 25% by using the camera upside down, and releasing the shutter from the underside.

Another off-beat camera design that will intrigue camera collectors is that of cameras that were made to look like binoculars, and take either single or stereoscopic pairs of pictures. The French variants of this design, called Photo-Jumelles, ranged from those that really looked like binoculars to some rather solid wedge-shaped boxes. These were popular in Europe from the 1890s up to the commencement of World War I. However, small cameras that were made after World War I will be easier for the collector to find.

There is a growing appreciation amongst collectors of the little oddball cameras that used their own special films. In 1937 the Coronet Camera Company introduced their Coronet Vogue. This was a lightweight, streamlined, bakelite novelty camera taking 30×50 mm pictures on its own special paper-backed 35 mm roll film

(Far left) Expo watch camera advertisement from the Photo-Miniature 1909.

The Ticka watch pocket camera, 'Every tick a picture.' The British version of the American Expo camera. Courtesy of The Kodak Museum.

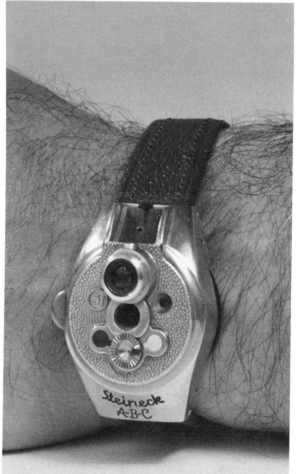

The Steinbeck ABC wristwatch camera took eight tiny exposures around a one inch diameter disc of film. Made in Germany, only a small number were sold. 1948.

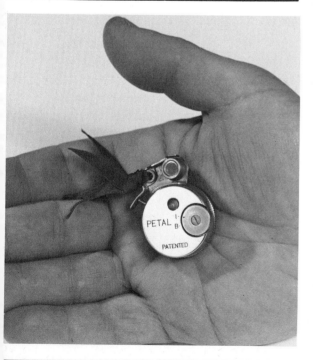

(Far left) The Petal camera made six tiny negatives around a disc of film. Two versions were produced in Japan. The round one shown here and an octagonal one the same size.

Made by the American Camera Co. of London, the Demon camera used $2\frac{1}{4}'' \times 2\frac{1}{4}''$ plates 1893. Courtesy of The Kodak Museum.

The Presto pocket camera made by E. B. Koopman of New York could hold four 30mm square plates or a roll of 30mm film, 1899. Courtesy of The Kodak Museum.

that was self-erecting at the touch of a button, though the springs on the one that I have are so strong that it explodes rather than opens! The Lumière Elgy and Super Elgy made in 1938, were French examples of this type of little camera. Measuring a minute $3'' \times 2'' \times 1\frac{3}{4}''$ and weighing only 7 oz., they made full-size 24×36 cm exposures on special eight exposure spools of 30 mm paper-backed roll film.

Collectors can classify these Elgy cameras by the 24×36 mm picture size, by the special roll film used, or by their extra small size. They show again how necessary it is to index and cross-index every camera as you collect.

The Ensign Midget was another tiny camera from this period. Sold by Ensign Limited, of 88–9 High Holborn, London, WC1, in 1934, it measured $1\frac{3}{4}'' \times 3\frac{5}{8}'' \times \frac{3}{4}''$, and was only $2\frac{1}{2}''$ deep when fully opened. It was designed along the lines of a miniature press camera, the front panel being supported very firmly on four struts. There was, in addition to the folding direct vision viewfinder, a brilliant viewfinder mounted on to the back of the lens panel, and the spool holders were on swivels, to allow easy loading. It was a precisely made little instrument, taking six exposures $1\frac{1}{4}'' \times 1\frac{5}{8}''$ on a size 10 (unperforated 35 mm) spool of film, and enlargements of up to $10'' \times 12''$ were often made from these small negatives. Collectors should look for the first two models that were made in 1934.

The Ensign Midget provides yet another opportunity for the collector to make a comprehensive collection of the varieties of a single camera and its accessories; and one that would not only combine the virtues of interest and inexpensiveness, but would also take up very little room at an exhibition or in a home.

As a contrast to these midget cameras which had been produced for the amateur

The Thornton-Pickard Snappa, a simple sliding box camera 1905.

market, the Minox sub-miniature was a really professional spy camera manufactured for secret agents and others engaged in espionage. Beautifully constructed, it was invented by Walter Zapp at Riga in Latvia, and was first made in 1935. Collectors should look for the original model of this cassette loading camera which can be distinguished by the twelve teeth on the take-up sprocket (from 1937, the take-up sprocket had only eight teeth). These pre-World War II cameras were made of chromium-plated brass and were really sturdy little jobs that produced first-class negatives. The cloak-and-dagger men of both the Allied and German intelligence services had these little cameras and made much use of them before and during World War II.

The Compass camera was in a class of its own, and is one of the cameras that every collector longs to find. It was designed by Noel Pemberton-Billing, an Englishman who had dreamed up the idea of a perfect camera and worked on its development from the early 1930s. It was a really well-thought-out camera, outstanding in its quality, and well ahead of its time. Manufactured in 1937 by the famous watchmaking firm of Le Coultre et Compagnie of Le Sentier, Switzerland, it had an $f3\cdot5$, 35 mm four-glass anastigmat lens especially designed and

made for it by Kern of Aarau, one of the top manufacturers of scientific optical instruments in Switzerland.

The Compass produced 24 × 36 mm negatives, using either single plates or cut films in special envelopes. A roll film back taking special six exposure spools was introduced in 1938, and although this increased the depth of the camera by less than $\frac{1}{8}''$ when in position, it was equipped with a semi-automatic film advance and a retractable pressure plate.

The Compass cameras in my collection include one complete with the original plate and film backs and another with the roll film back that was produced in England after World War II by T.A. Cubitt and Sons, of 2 Windmill Street, London W1. Improvements in cameras and lenses have made this camera obsolete, but when it was first made it was well ahead of its time, and it is a delightful item to have in a collection. I was interested to see one offered for sale to American collectors in January 1973 for $700 (£280), a price which shows the interest taken in these cameras in the United States.

The Steinbeck A.B.C. Wristwatch camera was another novelty camera that the collector will find fascinating. Made in Germany, it took eight exposures on a circular film and was extremely simple to use. The shutter speed was 1/125 of a second, and the fixed focus lens gave a sharp image of everything from 1·5 m to infinity. The only adjustment necessary was the diaphragm control, which was the knob on the front of the camera.

Although post-World War II cameras can hardly be called early cameras, many of the tiny sub-miniatures made then would be delightful additions to any collection. Cameras such as the Petie from West Germany, which took sixteen pictures 14 × 14 mm on a special roll of 16 mm film and had an instantaneous shutter (about 1/25 second) and an f 9 lens; or the Colly, a similar camera made by the Koeda Manufacturing Company in Japan, which took 14 × 14 mm pictures on 16 mm roll film, are good examples.

The Stylophot from France was a much more unusual camera. Shaped like a cigar, it was designed to be worn in the pocket like a fountain pen. Using 16 mm film supplied in cassettes of eighteen exposures it was light and compact, measuring $4\frac{1}{2}'' \times 1\frac{1}{2}'' \times 1''$.

'Smaller than a packet of cigarettes, the Minolta 16, hides in your pocket,' said the Minolta Camera Company Limited, of Osaka, Japan, when they introduced their Minolta 16 sub-miniature camera in 1954. Taking twenty 10 × 14 mm exposures on 16 mm film in daylight loading cassettes, it measured $3'' \times 1\frac{3}{4}'' \times 1''$ and weighed 6 oz.

Smaller still was the Petal camera, which was made in Japan soon after the end of World War II. This was loaded with a

Ensign Midget camera, film and enlarger 1934.

Eight sub-miniature cameras of the 1930's. These are rarely found today.

disc-like six-exposure magazine, and the only control gave the choice of instantaneous or bulb shutter speeds. Measuring $1\frac{1}{2}'' \times 1'' \times \frac{5}{8}''$ it is probably one of the smallest cameras ever made, and almost certainly the smallest that the collector will be able to find. Two versions were made, one with a hexagonal, and the other with a round body.

Many manufacturers have made novelties like the cigarette lighter camera, and these are welcomed by collectors as they add a happy note to collections. There is no name on the one in my collection, although both the lighter and camera work well. Because of this I have often wondered if it is just another novelty camera, or if it was really intended to be used by a spy.

Another camera which has historical associations is the Gelto 127. This roll film camera which dates from just after World War II, has engraved on its back the historic phrase 'made in occupied Japan'. A number of cameras were produced carrying this marking and these would make a thematic camera collection of great interest.

Small vest pocket cameras were very popular in the first half of the twentieth century and were made in great variety. The collector however should bear in mind that the term 'vest pocket' was often used by manufacturers as a general name for a camera that was made in several sizes.

The Sandco vest pocket camera made in 1914 could use plates in single metal slides, film pack, or with an adapter roll film. It was made in three sizes, $1\frac{1}{4}'' \times 2\frac{3}{8}''$, $2\frac{1}{2}'' \times 3\frac{1}{2}''$, and $3\frac{1}{4}'' \times 4\frac{1}{4}''$, and they were all called Sandco vest pocket cameras! Some vest pockets must have been very large indeed!

The title 'vest pocket camera' must have had considerable sales appeal, for we find lumped together in catalogues under that heading cameras such as the Watch Pocket

The camera is of course a cigarette lighter and the cigarette lighter a camera.

Cover of All British Photography *a catalogue of Ensign cameras and equipment which was over printed with the name of the retailer for local use 1923.*

The Stylophot from France was designed to be clipped into a pocket and worn like a fountain pen 1955.

Carbine ($2\frac{1}{4}'' \times 2\frac{1}{4}''$), the Ensignette ($1\frac{1}{2}'' \times 2\frac{1}{4}''$), the Vest Pocket Baby Sybil ($1\frac{3}{4}'' \times 2\frac{3}{8}''$), and many other odd sizes.

Many small Kodak cameras can of course be found for this type of collection. The roll film Pocket Kodak, taking pictures $1\frac{1}{2}'' \times 2''$ which was introduced in 1895, was the first of the small roll film cameras. The viewfinder on this camera had a circular field, and the fixed focus lens was fitted in an automatic instantaneous and time shutter.

During the early 1930s, Kodak took over the business of Dr Nagel, the famous camera designer, and amongst other Nagel cameras they marketed the Pupille in 1933.

Measuring only $3\frac{3}{4}'' \times 2\frac{5}{8}'' \times 1\frac{5}{16}''$, it took sixteen negatives $1'' \times 1\frac{3}{4}''$ (3×4 cm) on a roll of 127 Vest Pocket film, and there was a large choice of lenses, including Schneider Xenon $f\,2$, Zeiss Tessar $f\,2\cdot8$ and $f\,3\cdot5$, and Leitz Elmar $f\,3\cdot5$, in a compur shutter.

In the special 'Miniature Camera' issue of the *Amateur Photographer* published in the spring of 1935, twenty-eight miniature cameras taking pictures measuring $2\frac{1}{4}'' \times 2\frac{1}{4}''$ or smaller were listed. In a similar issue the following year, seventy-four different makes were reviewed, and there were several models of each make.

The Gelto 127 roll film camera has engraved on its back the historic phrase "Made in Occupied Japan".

Portable camera obscura used by Fox Talbot. Courtesy of The Science Museum.

IT'S ALL DONE WITH MIRRORS

THE earliest collectable cameras are the reflex camera obscuras that were first made at the end of the seventeenth century. During the eighteenth century the portable camera obscura became popular with that small section of the public that was educated enough to understand it, and affluent enough to afford it.

Collectors will find that reflex cameras from before the 1880s are few and far between. Although Thomas Sutton, then the editor of *Photographic Notes*, patented a single lens reflex camera in 1861, and the idea was put forward by several other inventors after this, it was not until the great upsurge of interest in photography that came in the 1880s with the advent of the dry plate, and in the 1890s with the introduction of roll films, that reflex cameras were really put on the market. Amongst the earliest that collectors will find are two British cameras: the Twin Lens Reflex was produced by R. and J. Beck Limited in 1880, a quarter-plate camera with both lenses moving at the same time; the Academy camera was made by Marion and Company in 1883. In the Academy camera which is the first twin-lens reflex

listed in the catalogue of the Science Museum Photography collection, both lenses move simultaneously when the image is focused on a ground glass screen. Some examples of this camera have the screen reflected in a mirror so as to give an upright image. These are amongst the earliest ancestors of today's twin lens reflex cameras. There are two examples of this camera in the Science Museum Photography Collection, the more usual quarter-plate size, and the rare miniature version which takes $1\frac{1}{4}'' \times 1\frac{1}{4}''$ plates. One of these small Academy cameras was sold for an amazing £651 ($1625) at Christie's sale in London on the 14th June 1973.

The American Patent Monocular Duplex, made in 1884, was one of the first single lens reflex cameras to be sold in any quantity. This American camera was advertised as the 'Artist's Camera' in the *British Journal Photographic Almanac* for 1886. Ross's New Portable Divided camera was another of the early twin lens reflex cameras that became popular in Britain in the 1890s, and before the end of the nineteenth century many manufacturers were making models of this sort.

Collectors will find that it is easier for

them to locate examples of the magazine twin lens reflex cameras which were made in great variety. From inexpensive cameras such as the 1897 Lancaster Zoegraph—a glorified box camera that cost £1.05 ($3) in a pocket version holding twelve $1\frac{5}{8}'' \times 2\frac{1}{8}''$ plates or cut films—right up to the half-plate Adams Twin Lens Camera de Luxe of 1893 which cost £38 ($152). This was a very considerable price in those days, but it was an outstanding camera. It was fitted with Goerz lenses, and aluminium sheaths, and the body, which measured $11'' \times 7\frac{5}{8}'' \times 9\frac{7}{8}''$ and weighed $7\frac{3}{4}$ lb., was covered with real black sealskin leather and bound in aluminium. Marketed also in quarter-plate and $4'' \times 5''$ sizes, they were advertised as 'the best and finest instrument it is possible to make'.

Single lens reflex cameras such as the one patented by Loman and made by Hinton and Company in London in 1896, and Shew's Reflector camera of 1897, which were simple to use and small in size compared with the twin lens reflex, soon came onto the market in increasing numbers, and by the early 1900s they were outselling the twin lens variety. The Cambier Bolton single lens reflex, made by W. Watson and Sons of London and Edinburgh, was another early example of this type of camera. Designed by Mr Cambier Bolton, who was a photographer of wild animals, it was planned with this purpose in mind and only long focus lenses could be used with it. It had a leather-covered mahogany body with a Thornton-Pickard focal plane shutter, and was made in the usual three sizes, quarter-

Portable camera obscura 1800,
(front and back.)

plate, 4″ × 5″, and half-plate.

J.F. Shew and Company were one of many manufacturers who made distinctive styles of cameras. No comprehensive collection of their cameras has yet been put together, although this would be a well worthwhile project for some collector. Their Popular Reflector, one of a series that started in 1899, was fitted with a flexible blind shutter.

In the early 1900s J.F. Shew and Company also produced the Focal Plane Reflector. This was fitted with a Goerz-Anschutz focal plane shutter with speeds of 1/25 to 1/1000 seconds and time, and had a reversible back, and rack and pinion focusing. Made in three sizes, quarter-plate, 4″ × 5″, and half-plate, a large number of different lenses were fitted to these cameras, besides the choice of twenty-one offered by the manufacturers.

The two half-plate Shew Press Reflec-

tors of 1903 were similar focal plane single lens reflex cameras, with triple extension, that were specially constructed to withstand rough use. But a more compact form of focal plane shutter was used in their Delta reflex camera of 1907, which had speeds of 1/10 to 1/2,500 seconds.

Focal plane shutters of several different types were by now available. On simple cameras the exposure time was adjusted by altering the speed at which the slit travelled

The London Stereoscopic Company's twin lens Artist hand camera advertisement 1894.

THE STEREOSCOPIC COMPANY'S TWIN LENS 'ARTIST' HAND CAMERA.

(PATENT.)

This Camera is especially recommended to those who prefer dark slides to an automatic plate changing arrangement. A separate focussing screen is supplied, so that the Camera can be used as an ordinary or stand camera when desired.

It is acknowledged to be unrivalled for Animal Photography.

It is used by the Principal Officers of H.M. Army and Navy because it

☛ Has a Finder the exact size of the plate you are using.
  Has Dark Slides of a novel description suitable for Plates or Films.
☛ Can be focussed even during the transition of the object to be photographed.
☛ Has an Instantaneous Shutter capable of various speeds, also time exposures.
☛ Can be used as a Hand Camera as well as on a stand for ordinary photography.
☛ It is fitted with exceptionally rapid lenses working at $f/6$.

Prices, complete with two Lenses and three Slides.

To take pictures 5 × 4 ... £15 15 0 | To take pictures 7½ × 5 ... £26 12 0
  ,,   ,,   6½ × 4¾... 25 0 0 | ,,   ,,   8½ × 6½... 35 0 0

EXTRA DARK SLIDES CAN BE HAD.

Price for Three 5×4 ... ... £1 17 6 | Price for Three 7½×5 ... ... £2 12 6
  ,,   ,,   ½-plates ... 2 5 0 | ,,   ,,   ½-plates ... 3 3 0

Send 9 Stamps for the Company's 200 page Catalogue.

THE LONDON STEREOSCOPIC AND PHOTOGRAPHIC CO., LTD.

106 AND 108 REGENT STREET, W., AND 54 CHEAPSIDE, E.C.

Ross of London made their first twin lens reflex in 1891. This is a later version 1902.

Early quarter plate twin lens reflex by Henry Park of London 1890. (Park worked for seven years with P. Meagher and eight with George Hare learning the trade before opening as a camera manufacturer himself, and his own cameras are very rare.)

across the film. Better ones were fitted with blinds that had adjustable slits, often the two blinds were used on two sets of rollers with the slits overlapping, the shutter speeds being adjusted by altering the amount of overlap. Although early front shutters are very collectable items, lending themselves to attractive displays, focal plane shutters are also of great interest to the collector.

Collectors with a historical bent will know that in 1907 the Folmer Graflex Corporation produced the first roll film single lens reflex cameras. Their IA model took $2\frac{1}{2}'' \times 4\frac{1}{4}''$ negatives on 116 film, and their 3A model $3\frac{1}{4}'' \times 5\frac{1}{2}''$ negatives on 112 film. Several other roll film models were marketed, including the National Graflex 1931 which took ten $2\frac{1}{4}'' \times 2\frac{1}{2}''$ negatives on 120 film. Aside from these however, most Graflex cameras will be found with a variety of backs, so that they could be used with plates, cut film, film packs, or roll films.

The reflex Premograph, made in 1910, a simpler single lens reflex that came from the Kodak stable, used quarter-plate film packs. Only costing £2.10 ($8.25) with an $f8$ Bausch and Lomb lens, the same key was used to set the mirror and make the exposure.

The Butcher Reflex Carbine, made in 1922, was another straightforward single lens reflex designed for the amateur market. Focusing was by means of a knob on top of the camera that moved the lens in and out on the end of a tiny round bellows, and the shutter and mirror were both set by the movement of a lever in front of the hood. After the amalgamation of Houghtons Limited with the camera's manufacturers, W. Butcher and Sons, on 1st January 1926, its production was continued as the Carbine Roll Film Reflex $2\frac{1}{4}$B. The Ensign Roll Film Reflex was the same camera fitted with a taller hood, this being 8″ high instead of 4″. Collectors should not overlook these simpler amateur cameras. They add

Newman and Guardia quarter plate twin lens reflex 1894.

Loman's patent quarter plate single lens reflex 1896.

breadth to the usual vertical progression of a collection, as well as providing a muted background for the more exotic and outstanding cameras in a display.

Newman and Guardia Limited have been producing many collectable cameras

3A GRAFLEX

since 1891 and their Reflex was one of their outstanding models. A 'new' camera by collecting standards, it was first introduced in 1921, and was still being sold in 1957. Made in one film size only, $2\frac{1}{2}'' \times 3\frac{1}{2}''$, it measured $5\frac{3}{4}'' \times 6'' \times 3\frac{1}{2}''$, and weighed 3 lb. 3 oz. The body was made of duralumin covered with leather, and featured a revolving back, and a rising, falling and horizontal swing front. It could be used with Newman and Guardia double book form metal slides, single metal slides, film pack adapter, roll film holder, or changing box.

For generations Adams and Company made and sold cameras and photographic equipment in London. In the nineteenth century much of it was made in the Steam Factory of which they were so proud. Of all the cameras that they produced, the one that

Premograph single lens reflex. Rochester Optical Company advertisement 1907.

they would probably pick out for a collection is their Studio Minex, made in 1927, which they called 'the most perfect studio camera ever invented'.

Two years ago I paid £10 ($25) for a half-plate Studio Minex and stand in mint condition. Although it would bring much more than that today, it is typical of the bulky cameras that are too obsolete to have any commercial value, while still not being old enough to have any great historical value to most collectors. This type of camera can still be purchased quite reasonably, and looks lovely in a collection.

A group of the miniature reflex cameras produced by Franke and Heidecke of Braunschweig in Germany would provide collectors with an interesting example of camera evolution. Their designer, Dr Reinhold Heidecke, was an amateur photographer and he conceived the idea of a small-sized stereoscopic reflex camera, and made his first prototype in 1908. After World War I, he obtained the backing of Paul Franke, and the firm they created, Franke and Heidecke, produced its first camera, the Heidoscope stereoscopic plate camera, in 1921. This was to be the forerunner of a series of miniature reflex cameras that were to become ranked amongst the best loved and most popular cameras in the world, and which were followed by a host of imitators.

The Heidoscope, which was made in two sizes 45×107 mm and 6×13 cm, was a true reflex camera, having a third lens for the viewfinder positioned between the two taking lenses, this arrangement solving any problem of parallax. In order to obtain a bright field of view, an $f\,4{\cdot}2$ lens was fitted and the image was reflected by a mirror on to a ground glass screen protected by the now well-known Rollei folding hood. The Rolleidoscope, made in 1924, was a roll film version of this camera using 127 Vest Pocket film in the smaller and 120 film in the larger version.

Several versions were made of both sizes of the Rolleidoscope, with both external and internal modifications. There were variations in the shutter and of the position of the shutter tensioning lever on the Heido-

Butcher's roll film Reflex Carbine 1922.

151

This Newman and Guardia folding single lens reflex with its highly polished wooden front gleaming brass lens panel red leather covered body and black leather hood is an outstanding camera for the collector 1921.

scope (in later models on top of the camera instead of the front). Earlier models of the Rolleidoscope can be recognized as they have only two film rollers in the back, later models having an additional third roller at the centre of the back, on the rear of the septum. These later models also had the edges of the pressure plate bent forward so as to provide guides for the film. I have seen these cameras advertised recently at up to £200 ($500) each, but there is no need for collectors to pay a lot of money for any of these cameras from the 1920s and 1930s. They were mostly made in fairly large quantities, and being quality cameras have been well preserved.

The decision to produce the Rolleiflex, a twin lens reflex of the same style as the Rolleidoscope stereoscopic camera, must have been taken in 1925 as Franke and Heidecke have estimated that it took about three years to put this new camera into production. The first Rollei was fitted with an $f4·5$ Zeiss Tessar lens with a 24 mm mount diameter in a compur shutter with speed of from 1 to 1/300 seconds, bulb and time. The viewfinder hood had a hinged mirror that could be set at 45 degrees for eye-level focusing. This first Rolleiflex is the hardest for the collector to find as it was made for a shorter period than any of the other models, but it was a popular camera that sold well and still shows up from time to time. I recently bought one in first-class condition for £5 from a friendly camera dealer.

A second model was introduced a year later, in 1929, and was identical to the first except for the lenses. An $f3·8$ tessar was substituted for the original $f4·5$ lens, and an $f3·1$ for the viewfinder lens, giving a much brighter image and easier focusing. This use of a finder lens which was faster than the taking lens was to become standard Rollei practice, and the Rolleiflex Standard of 1932 came with a choice of an $f4·5$ or $f3·8$ tessar

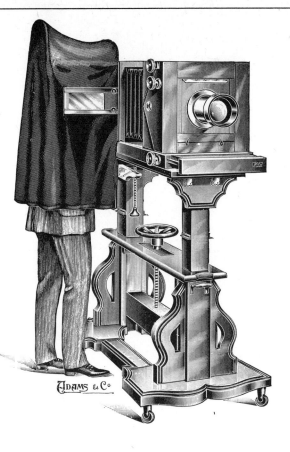

lens in the compur shutter, and the faster *f* 3·1 finder lens. Another improvement in this model was the use of a single lever to both cock and release the shutter instead of the two separate levers used on earlier models.

The fourth camera in the Rollei quartet was the Rolleicord of 1933. This was a less expensive camera. The body was metal plated and a framefinder was incorporated in the viewfinder hood.

In 1931 a smaller version of the Rolleiflex was produced, using 127 vest pocket size film. The first few of these smaller Rolleiflex cameras were called Babyflex, and these are very rare indeed. I have never seen one, and I don't know of any collector who has one. The name was soon changed to Sports Rolleiflex and all subsequent versions of the vest pocket model have used this name.

Many more models of the Rollei have been made, but unless the collector wishes to specialize in them and gather together a complete set of all the different models that have been made it is really the first few that should be looked for.

The Pilot folding twin lens reflex was another most interesting miniature reflex camera. This was introduced into England in 1932 by its makers, Guthe and Thorsch of Dresden, who also made the famous Patent Étui which they claimed was the thinnest camera in the world—the $2\frac{1}{2}'' \times 3\frac{1}{2}''$ model was only $\frac{5}{8}''$ thick when closed. The Pilot they claimed, was 'the world's smallest reflex'. It sold well on the Continent but is comparatively scarce in England and the United States. It measured $5'' \times 3\frac{1}{2}'' \times 2''$ overall when closed and was only $2\frac{3}{4}''$ thick when fully open. The taking lens extended on bellows, and the viewing lens on telescopic metal tubes. The front and the hood were self-erecting at the touch of a button, the hood contained a magnifier, and there was an eye-level viewfinder on the side. Two models were made, both using 127 roll film.

A group of all seven versions of this camera would take some putting together, but is certainly worth doing. Attempting to gather such a collection together is what makes camera collecting so interesting and exciting.

In 1936 Guthe and Thorsch also made a single lens reflex, the Pilot 6. In 1938 the Pilot 6 was fitted with an improved shutter with seven speeds. The Pilot Super 6 took six photographs $3\frac{1}{4}'' \times 3\frac{1}{4}''$ on a roll film made for them by Perutz. However, at a time when the trend was towards smaller cameras, a new larger format with a bulkier camera, using an unusual film size that many dealers did not stock, had little chance of success, and production soon ceased. This makes the Pilot Super 6 the most rare Pilot of them all and a real collector's camera. These Pilot single lens reflex cameras could be subjoined to a collection of Pilot folding twin lens reflex cameras, or kept in orderly progres-

*Franke and Heidecke's
Heidoscop stereoscopic
plate camera 1921.*

*The Rolleidoscop was the roll
film version of the Heidoscop.
They both had the now familiar
Rollei folding view finder hood,
1924. (The names were spelled
both with and without a
terminal 'e'.)*

The original Rolleiflex of 1928 had an f4.5 Zeiss Tessar lens and took six pictures $2\frac{1}{4}'' \times 2\frac{1}{4}''$ on 117 roll film, 1928.

sion with the other single lens reflexes in the collection.

There are fashions in camera collecting as there are in all kinds of collecting, and the popularity of different types or makes of cameras waxes and wanes. The reflex camera that has kept its interest longest amongst collectors, and the one that holds a place in the collector's heart equivalent to that held by the Leica and Contax amongst the rangefinder cameras, is the Exakta.

Ihagee of Dresden had been manufacturing single lens reflex cameras for many years when they introduced the Exakta Vest Pocket Model A. Production of this camera started in 1931. They were first marketed in Great Britain in 1933, and in the United States in 1936. The same year a Vest Pocket Exakta Junior was also marketed. This had a non-interchangeable lens and was possibly the forerunner of the post-war Exa series of cameras. Collectors should watch for the plate back model which was produced in 1937. This was a Model B modified to take plates and cut films, and examples are few and far between.

In 1937 the original Exakta 66 was produced. This camera was the same shape as the Vest Pocket Exaktas, but much larger, taking 6×6 cm (2¼″×2¼″) negatives on 120 roll film. The film was wound on by pushing a 5″ long lever, which was pivoted under the front of the camera, twice across the camera. As in all these Exaktas, the film transport mechanism also wound the shutter, and brought the reflex mirror into position. Later versions were made fitted with 80 mm *f* 3·5 tessar lenses, and a second model, marketed in 1939, had a shorter 3″ film transport lever which was only moved once across the camera and back, and a full range of twenty-six speeds. The war interrupted production of this camera, and it is now one of the rarer Exaktas. I know of only three in all of Britain.

The first Rolleicord was metal plated and used 120 roll film, 1933.

As happened in so many cases, it was the smaller size models that dominated the market, and the outstanding success of the Exakta range was the Kine Exakta that first appeared in 1936. This remarkable little camera is a 'must' for the collector. It was the first 35 mm single lens reflex, the first to have speeds from 1/1,000 to 12 seconds, the first with built-in synchronization, and the first 35 mm camera with a lever wind film advance. Its die-cast metal alloy body was of a similar shape to the Vest Pocket Exaktas and, like them, it had a self-capping focal plane shutter and interchangeable lenses. A few of the early model 2s were marked Exacta, and these are the ones to look for, as since them the name has always been spelt with a 'k'. The post-war Kine Exakta Model 2, made in 1949, was very similar, but did not have the inching-on action of the earlier version. This was the last Exakta to use Kine as part of its name. These 35 mm models were

The second version of the Pilot folding twin lens reflex 1933.

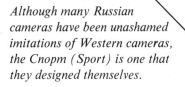

called Kine Exaktas to differentiate them from the earlier Vest Pocket Exaktas using 127 film.

The Exakta was one of the earliest cameras to have a complete system built around it. The range of the equipment is among the most comprehensive available to the collector and is too extensive to list here. Its value is added to by the fact that, contrary to the practice of many manufacturers, the Exakta was designed so as not to become obsolete. So much so that many of their modern lenses will fit the 1936 Kine Exakta, numbers of which are still giving satisfactory service today.

Camera collecting is still a new enough hobby for it to be the answer to a collector's dream. Although prices have risen rapidly during the last couple of years, it is still possible to buy examples of interesting cameras such as these pre-war Exaktas at reasonable prices and I recently paid £5 ($12.50) for an excellent early example of the Kine Exakta. This opportunity to buy, at rock bottom prices, cameras, in which no one is as yet interested, is something collectors will envy in the future.

Voigtländer have made cameras since the earliest days of photography and the Voigtländer Superb is well worth a place in

one dated 1937 illustrated in the *Daguerrian Era* catalogue No. 2 for Fall 1971. Fitted with the *f* 2·8 tessar lens, it was priced at £98 ($245). At this rate, these second-hand thirty-five-year-old cameras will soon cost more now than they did when new! (Fitted with the *f* 2·8 tessar lens they cost $267 in the United States when they were first marketed.)

The Reflex Korelle, made in 1936, was another trendsetting camera. Similar in design to the Noviflex which had been marketed a year earlier, the Korelle was a much better camera altogether. It was a much copied camera and collectors should try and find an example before they also become fashionable, and their prices rocket.

Lenses supplied with the Korelle included some of the finest Zeiss Tessars and Schneider Xenars available. On earlier models these were 75 mm focal length, but on later ones 80 mm lenses were fitted. The camera body was made of aluminium covered with morocco leather, with chromium trim and fittings.

Whilst Korelle cameras were ideal for standard and telephoto lenses, wide angle lenses could not be used on them. The distance from the lens flange to the film plane was 75 mm (3″) and the lenses could not be recessed into the body of the camera as they would interfere with the working of the mirror. Korelles were, however, offered with a very large choice of lenses, and the collector should not be surprised at any off-beat ones that are found fitted.

Collectors will value the Welta Perfekta and Superfekta folding twin lens reflex cameras for their unusual shape and design. Made by the Welta Kamera Werke GmbH, Freital, Germany, they were both fitted with *f* 3·8 Zeiss Tessar lenses in compur shutters and used 120 film. They were attractive and well-made cameras, the one to really look for being the larger

any collection. Taking the usual twelve $2\frac{1}{4}''$ square negatives on 120 film it had a 3″ Voigtländer Skopar *f* 3·5 lens in a compur shutter fitted with delayed action. Amongst its attractive features was a little prism mounted on the front of the compur shutter to allow the speeds to be seen when looking down from the top of the camera. It also had a most unusual method of combating parallax. A lever moving below the taking lens focused both the lenses, simultaneously tilting the viewfinder lens downwards so that the picture seen on the screen was exactly the same as that taken on the film at any distance from 3′ to infinity.

The Zeiss Ikon Contaflex, made in 1935, is a much sought after collector's camera of great interest. It was the first 35 mm twin lens reflex ever made and was also the very first camera to have a built-in photo-electric exposure meter. With a coupled shutter and film wind, interchangeable taking lenses (six were available), the well-tried Contax metal focal plane shutter speeded from $\frac{1}{2}$ to 1/1,000 seconds and time, and a delayed action device, it was a really new concept in cameras.

Although these Contaflex cameras had very little commercial value a few years ago, competition amongst collectors has now pushed the prices up. I was interested to see

(Far left) The Voigtlander Superb $2\frac{1}{4}'' \times 2\frac{1}{4}''$ twin lens reflex had a unique system of parallax compensation and unusual reversed engraving of the speeds on its compur shutter which are seen from above in a little prism. 1933.

The Zeiss Ikon Contaflex was the first 35mm twin lens reflex, and the first camera with a built in photo-electric exposure meter, 1935. It is now an extremely expensive collector's camera.

The Welta Superfecta $2\frac{1}{4}'' \times 3\frac{1}{4}''$ folding twin lens reflex is one of the very few that were made in that size, 1935.

$2\frac{1}{4}'' \times 3\frac{1}{4}''$ Superfekta as very few twin lens reflex cameras were made in that size. This camera boasted a revolving back that permitted the film to be turned to a horizontal position, and automatically reversed a mask under the viewing screen to show the correct shape of the picture.

The Zeiss Ikon Ikoflex is another camera that the collector can, as it were, watch evolving. As originally marketed in Great Britain in 1934 it was an inexpensive twin lens reflex taking twelve exposures, $2\frac{1}{4}'' \times 2\frac{1}{4}''$, on roll film and had a die-cast body and lever focusing.

In 1936 a new model, the Ikoflex II, was introduced. With straighter sides, altered lens panel, chrome plating, there was a choice of an $f\,3\cdot5$ Zeiss Tessar or Triotar lenses in compur or compur rapid shutters. The model called the Ikoflex I that was introduced into the United States in 1938 was very similar to this Ikoflex II.

The European Ikoflex III, made in 1938, was another model with only slight improvements, but the Ikoflex III marketed in America in 1939 was a very different camera indeed. It had a different lens panel and was the only Ikoflex with a film transport lever and an Albada sportsfinder.

The Photographic Dealer's Association's *Monark Price Guide* lists twelve varieties of the Ikoflex, valued at from £3 to £19 ($7 to $47), and I am sure that by hunting around a collector could put together a complete series of them at no great expense.

At the beginning of World War II most of the top grade cameras available in Great Britain were purchased by the government for use by the armed forces. This caused a shortage of precision cameras and as a direct result several manufacturers began to produce cameras that were based on the now unobtainable continental models. For instance the Aeronautical and General

Instrument Company (Agilux Limited) of Croydon made a copy of the Reflex Korelle for the Royal Navy. Called the 'A.G.I.' Reflex, this camera handled and felt like a battleship, and was so solidly built that it was almost bullet-proof.

Reid and Sigrist Limited, of Leicester, produced the Reid 35 mm high precision rangefinder cameras which were copied almost exactly from the Leica cameras. The Reid I and IA had no rangefinder. The Reid II had a coupled rangefinder but no slow speeds, and the Reid III was a replica of the Leica IIIb with built in flash synchronization. Although outdated these cameras have retained their value, and command higher prices today than the Leicas that they were copied from.

The Microflex and Microcord twin lens reflex cameras, produced by Micro Precision Products Limited of Kingston upon Thames, were modelled almost screw for screw on Franke and Heidecke's Rolleis and are another example of a first-class product that has kept its value, costing as much or more today as the Rolleis that they were copied from.

Many important collections of these copy cameras have been put together, copy Leicas being the most popular, and it is a fascinating field for the new collector to specialize in.

Several other interesting reflex cameras were made in Great Britain in the years after the war. Wray (Optical Works) Limited, who were established in the year that Fox Talbot first brought photography into existence, produced the Wrayflex in 1951. This was off-beat enough to satisfy any collector giving as it did an upside down image in the viewfinder and a negative 24 × 32 mm, on standard 35 mm film.

Finally, collectors will find delight in what are probably the two smallest reflex cameras ever made. Produced during the post-war surge of interest in sub-miniature cameras, the smallest twin lens reflex was the Goerz Minicord, made in 1952. Produced by G.P. Goerz, in Vienna, it took forty exposures 10 mm square on a cassette load of 16 mm film using reloadable twin container cassettes, and measured a tiny $4'' \times 2\frac{3}{4}'' \times 1\frac{1}{8}''$.

The smallest single lens reflex was the 16 mm Russian Narcissus. This had a focal plane shutter with speeds of 1/30 to 1/500 seconds, and interchangeable lenses. With suitable adapters most of the lenses designed for the Russian Zenith cameras could also be used.

No account of collectable reflex cameras would be complete without a mention of that outstanding example of reflex cameras, the Hasselblad. The first Model 1600 appeared in 1948, and was fitted with a Kodak Ektra lens (Hasselblad were Kodak's Swedish agent). One day it will be an important camera for collectors, and think what a glorious item one of the Space Hasselblads that have been to the moon would be if a collector could only get hold of one.

The copy of the Reflex Korelle made during World War II for the British Navy by A.G.I. was built like a battleship and was practically bullet proof.

The original Wrayflex of 1951 is a collectable camera because of its unusual 24 × 32 mm negative size and its viewfinder which gives an inverted image.

The 1000 F. Hasselblad first introduced in 1954 (front and back).

Stereoscopic daguerreotype of the Great Exhibition at the Crystal Palace, London, 1851. A similar stereoscopic daguerreotype was sold on the 8th March 1974 at Sotheby's for £440 ($1,100) but a friend of mine bought another example of this scene in March 1975 for £15 ($36)!

STEREOSCOPIC CAMERAS

FOR collectors, the happy coincidence of the almost simultaneous invention of the stereoscope by Sir Charles Wheatstone in 1838 and the announcement a few months later of the invention of photography by Daguerre and Fox Talbot, seems too good to be true. If ever two inventions complemented each other, it was these. Wheatstone had the first stereoscope constructed in 1832 and continued his experiments intermittently for several years. The Royal Society published his paper 'Some Remarkable and hitherto Unobserved Phenomena of Binocular Vision', in their *Philosophical Transactions* of 1838. These Wheatstone reflecting stereoscopes are the earliest items of collectable stereoscopic equipment, but I know of none outside museums.

During the early 1840s stereoscopic pairs of photographs were taken using both the calotype and daguerreotype processes. These early stereoscopic photographs are now of the utmost rarity. They were made by sequential exposures. A photograph was taken, the camera moved 2″ or 3″ to one side, and then the second photograph was taken. At first the cameras were often moved as much as 5″ or 6″ apart on the principle that if a little was good a lot was better! It was soon found however that this caused gross distortion, and a distance of about $2\frac{1}{2}″$ to 3″ became a standard.

Still-life pictures were more successful than portraits because it was difficult for anyone to keep perfectly still for long enough to have two almost identical photo-

graphs taken. Two cameras were sometimes used side by side, and by 1842 improvements in the daguerreotype process and in camera lenses cut the time of exposures from as much as thirty minutes to thirty seconds.

The first real improvement in stereoscopic viewing was Sir David Brewster's box type refracting stereoscope of 1849. This type of stereoscope was a great advance, and the approximately $3\frac{1}{2}'' \times 7''$ slide that it used was to become the first standard size for stereograms.

Stereoscopic photography was at first just another scientific curiosity, and it was not until the Great Exhibition in London in 1851 that it became really popular. Queen Victoria so admired the sets of daguerreotype stereoscopic slides and Brewster viewers exhibited by Jules Duboscq that a special viewer and set of slides were made and presented to her. This was just the push that stereoscopy needed and it was to become one of the leading forms of photography for many years.

The stereoscope became very popular in the early 1850s; they were first introduced into the United States in 1850, the earliest ones being Brewster and Combination type viewers imported from France and many manufacturers started to produce them. Early models of the Brewster stereoscope can be identified because, until Claudet patented his improved version in 1855, they had no provision for focusing the lenses or for varying their interocular separation. However it should be remembered that cheaper versions without these improvements continued to be produced for many years. Claudet's patent included his invention the cabinet viewer, with the slides carried on moving bands. Later models of this had two pairs of lenses so that two people could view at the same time. These are not easy to find today, but examples of

Brewster type stereoscope 1860, made of laquered wood.

most types of early stereoscopes are still relatively easy to come across. An exception is the stereoscopic daguerreotype case. It was first patented in England by W.E. Kilburn in January 1853 and Claudet patented his own version two months later. A similar design was patented the same month in America by J.F. Mascher of Philadelphia and a slightly different one by John Stull, also of Philadelphia, in February 1855. Although the idea was pirated by other manufacturers—I have an exact copy of the Kilburn case without a manufacturer's name in my collection—they are very scarce now, few having survived the 120 years or so since they were manufactured.

Stereoscopic daguerreotype slides are another example of rare early stereoscopic items which are well worth looking for. They were soon replaced by the glass, and then by the card stereograms that became so popular, and are now extremely rare and costly, outstanding examples having recently fetched as much as £1,600 ($3,840).

Other interesting early types of viewers for a collection are the various forms of folding combination graphoscopes and pantascopes which were made from the early 1850s right up to World War I. One interesting model incorporated a folding Brewster-type box. Many folding-type pocket models were made and, again, earlier viewers can be distinguished by the slots used for adjusting the position of the card instead of the sliding card holder which was first introduced in 1861.

In 1859 the English firm Smith, Beck and Beck began to sell very fine stereoscopes. Their New Achromatic Stereoscope and Patent Mirror Stereoscope both won world renown. The Patent Mirror Stereoscope was designed for examining stereograms in books as well as for viewing cards and transparencies, and were made in both hand and stand models. They were probably the finest instruments of their type produced in that period, and are wonderful collectors' pieces.

The next real improvement in the stereoscope came from the United States in 1860. Oliver Wendel Holmes devised the skeletal hand-viewer which was to become universally used, and it was first produced by Joseph L. Bates in Boston in 1861. These first Holmes hand stereoscopes had fixed card holders with grooves across them to allow the stereograms to be placed nearer or further from the lenses to allow for differences in vision, and a fixed handle, which was originally a bradawl just pushed into the wood. Bates made a modified version with a sliding card holder and a folding handle, and millions of these were sold all over the world. In England it was called the American Stereoscope as a tribute to its inventor.

Holmes stereoscopes are still very common in antique shops and markets, and collectors should look for the more unusual versions that were made. The easiest of these to find are those on a turned wood table stand, either as a combined piece or

as a separate stand and viewer. Collectors should look out for Brewster-type viewers on table stands, as these are more rare than the ordinary hand models. One lovely example of these that I have has statuettes of the 'Three Graces' around the base of the stand.

More interesting to the collector, and harder to find, are the chests and boxes holding single or pairs of viewers and a selection of stereograms. One box in my collection has a secret compartment where presumably Papa hid his stereograms of nude ladies.

The Swan's Stereoscopic Treasury of 1860 is another very rare and lovely example. A walnut chest measuring $9'' \times 7'' \times 5\frac{5}{8}''$, it contains a delicate Swan's hand stereoscope, made of matching walnut trimmed with red plush, and seventy stereograms. The stereograms in the excellent Treasury in my collection date from 1859 and include fine pierced and coloured tissues of that year and instantaneous views of Paris dated 1865, all in mint condition.

The first binocular camera was made by John Benjamin Dancer of Manchester in 1853. It was a box-type camera measuring $8\frac{1}{4}'' \times 7\frac{1}{2}'' \times 5''$, and weighing about 3 lb. The lenses were $4\frac{1}{4}''$ $f 5\cdot3$ doublets spaced $3''$ apart, and focusing was by a rack and pinion. $3\frac{1}{4}'' \times 6\frac{3}{4}''$ plates were used in single dark slides and the shutter was two brass lens caps joined by a strip of wood. Treasured for nearly a hundred years, this camera was destroyed by bombs during an air raid on Manchester during World War II. But one made by Dancer in 1856 is in the Science Museum in London where a folding binocular stereoscopic camera made in 1857 by Meagher, the well-known London camera manufacturer, can also be seen.

Stereoscopic pairs of photographs were still being taken with single lens cameras and special single lens stereoscopic cameras were still being made for many years after that. Powell's single lens stereoscopic camera made in 1858 by Horne and Thornthwaite of Newgate Street, London, is an

*Folding Graphoscope 1865
(open and closed).*

outstanding example. It was one of the earliest cameras to use Waterhouse stops which were introduced in that year.

Well known as opticians and instrument makers, Horne, Thornthwaite and Wood were first mentioned in the London Directory for 1844. By 1858, when they made the Powell's single lens stereoscopic camera, Mr Wood was no longer with them, and they were listed as Horne and Thornthwaite, Opticians, Philosophical and Photographic Instrument Makers in Ordinary to Her Majesty, Manufacturers of Chemical and Mathematical Instruments, and Sole Makers of Blundell's Patent Apparatus for the Abstraction of Teeth. From 1886 until 1893, they were Horne, Thornthwaite and Wood again, and from 1894 to 1913 when they were last listed, they were known once more as Horne and Thornthwaite. Established first at 123 Newgate Street, in the City of London, they gradually expanded to No. 122 and by 1858 to No. 121. They moved in 1875 to 3 Holburn Viaduct, from 1876 onwards they were at 416 The Strand, and in the 1880s they had additional premises at 74 Cheapside. Information of this sort, the result of patient research, is of great help in the dating of early cameras. Collectors should keep careful notes of any such particulars that come their way.

Another collectors' gem from this firm was their triple lens stereoscopic camera. This camera had a movable metal plate immediately behind the lens panel with a pair of apertures for the two outside lenses and a single one for the centre lens about $1\frac{1}{2}''$ higher. When this plate was pushed down as far as possible it covered the two outside lenses, allowing light to pass through the single central lens, reach the sensitized plate and make a single photograph. When it was lifted upwards, it obscured the central lens and uncovered the outside lenses for stereoscopic photography. Used

Beck Beck and Smith's 'New Achromatic Stereoscope' 1858. Courtesy of The Howarth -Loomes Collection.

in conjunction with the appropriate lens cap or caps, this must have been an efficient shutter mechanism for exposing the slow wet plates then in use.

The label on this camera bears the legend Horne and Thornthwaite 121, 122 and 123 Newgate Street. This, together with the fact that the centre lens used Waterhouse stops, dates this camera as having been made between 1858, when they expanded to No. 121 from Nos 122 and 123, and 1874, when the firm moved from this address. Both of these cameras are extremely rare.

Any item from this period is of course very scarce, and when it is realized that one camera was used to produce thousands of stereograms, which were in turn reproduced for use in millions of viewers, the importance of these early cameras can be easily understood, and the locating of one becomes a most exciting event to the collector. A wet

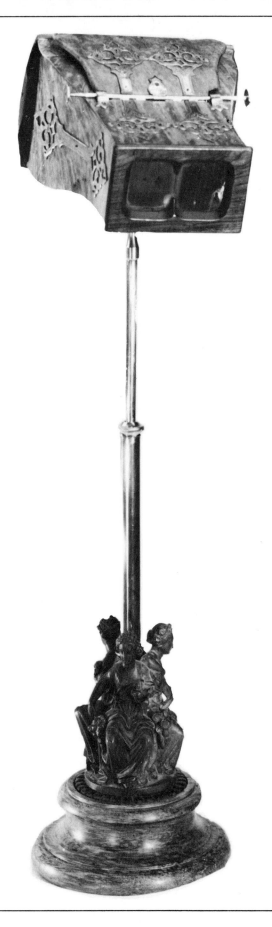

plate camera made by Morley of London in 1860 with a pair of Negretti and Zambra lenses, one wet slide, and a packet of stereo pictures was sold for £851 ($2,127) at the Christie's sale on 14th June 1973. This was then the highest price that had ever been paid in Great Britain for an antique camera, and although this was an exceptional example it gives some idea of the value of these early cameras today.

The first book to be illustrated with stereoscopic photographs was *Teneriffe, an Astronomer's Experiment* by C. Piazzi Smith. Published in London in 1858, *Teneriffe* is now a real collector's classic. Although copies could be bought for a few pounds only a little while ago, prices have risen in line with those of most other items of interest to camera collectors, and copies in good condition are now fetching prices in the region of £100 ($240). The second book of this type, *The Conway in the Stereoscope*, published in 1860, was illustrated with twenty beautiful sepia-toned stereograms (real pictures were used in each copy) taken by Roger Fenton.

Millions of stereograms were produced all over the world until the 1860s when the carte-de-visite photograph superseded the stereoscope in the public's fancy. From the second half of the nineteenth century until well into the twentieth stereograms were profitably exhibited to the public by means of the Kalloscop penny-in-the-slot stereoscopic viewers in amusement arcades and at seaside piers. The Kalloscop in my collection was hand-crafted and was one of a pair that I located some time ago. But though interest in the stereoscope waned until the 1880s it did not entirely die away and the dry plate process brought new life to all types of photography. There was soon a spate of cameras using the new process, which benefited amateurs and professionals alike and left a legacy of glittering brass and glass for collectors today. Meagher's $3\frac{1}{4}'' \times 6\frac{3}{4}''$ stereo

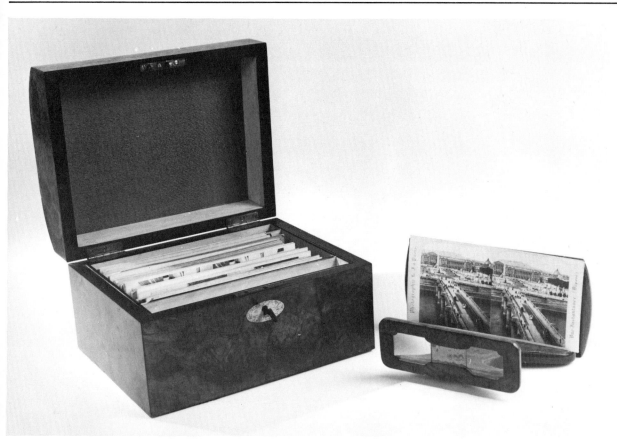

Swan's Stereoscopic Treasury 1860. One of these elegant outfits was sold at Christies on 14th December 1972 for £79 ($197) and would fetch much more than that now.

camera; the Lancaster $3\frac{1}{4}'' \times 6\frac{3}{4}''$ stereo camera; and the stereoscopic Lizar's Challenge, are perhaps typical examples of these wooden cameras and many of the ordinary half-plate cameras then on sale could be purchased with an extra twin lens front panel and septum for stereoscopic photographs.

Collectors will also find many stereoscopic versions of the magazine cameras that were so popular in the 1890s and 1900s. Ensign's stereo Klyto is a good example of these. It held twelve $3\frac{1}{4}'' \times 6\frac{3}{4}''$ dry plates, and its magazine worked in the same way as that of its single lens brother.

Another most interesting and rare item for a collection of stereoscopic equipment is the Ives Kromscop first made in 1892. (Louis Walton Sipley in his *Collector's Guide to American Photography* describes the Kromscop as the 'rarest of 19th century stereoscopes'.) Frederic Eugene Ives had many inventions to his credit in the field of photography but this is the most collectable of them all. His Kromscop was the first natural colour stereoscopic viewer. The negatives were made using a repeating back with red, green and blue filters. When the three pairs of two dimensional monochrome pictures were viewed with this wonderful device a perfectly coloured three-dimensional image was seen.

The Kromscop in my collection was a gift, and although it is extremely rare every collector to whom I have mentioned it seems to have one! Nevertheless I had not seen one for sale, nor been offered one privately in nearly twenty years of collecting cameras, until two appeared in the summer of 1973. The first—in excellent condition—was sold at Sotheby's on the 24th May 1973 for £160; the second—not as nice—was sold at Christie's three weeks later, on the 14th June 1973, for £220. These prices are yet another indication of the increasing popularity of camera collecting.

J. B. Dancer of Manchester made this, the first twin lens stereoscopic camera, not later than 1853. This model was not patented. (H. Garnett and C. H. Oakden, – "The Original Binocular Stereoscopic Camera of John Benjamin Dancer", – in "Proceedings of the Seventh International Congress of Photography, London," July 9-14, 1928.

Twin lens stereoscopic camera patented by J. B. Dancer in 1856. Courtesy of The Science Museum.

*Meagher's folding
stereoscopic camera, 1857.
Courtesy of The Science
Museum.*

Collectors should also look for examples of the Ives Parallax Stereogram, first made in 1903. These were the precursors of the modern lenticular stereoscopic print, and are also choice items for a collection.

As in so many other fields of photography, the advent of the Kodaks brought about a rebirth of public interest in stereoscopy. The first Kodak stereoscopic camera was called the Stereo Weno Hawkeye, made in 1902. This had a pair of rapid rectilinear lenses, and a Bausch and Lomb shutter. The Stereo Hawkeye No. 1 of 1904 had a Stereo Automatic shutter (time, instantaneous and bulb) with 5″ rapid rectilinear lenses, and the Stereo Hawkeye No. 2 was fitted with $5\frac{3}{4}″$ extra rapid rectilinear lenses, a Bausch and Lomb Automatic Stereo shutter speeded from 1 to 1/100 seconds, time and bulb, and had the added refinement of a rising front. All three cameras used 118 film. In the following years six more models were produced.

The No. 2 Stereo Kodak made in 1901 adds a nice touch of variety to this series of stereoscopic cameras. It was a box camera using 101 film with rapid rectilinear lenses and a Special Stereo shutter. The No. 2 Stereo Brownie, produced four years later and fitted with a pair of meniscus achromatic lenses in a Brownie Automatic shutter, was another folding camera.

In 1917 the Stereo Kodak No. 1 was brought out fitted with a pair of Kodak anastigmat f 7.7 lenses and a Stereo Automatic shutter. An updated version introduced two years later had a Stereo No. 2 Ball Bearing shutter. Accessories available for these cameras were a black or tan carrying case, a stereo Kodak self-transposing frame,

and Kodak portrait attachments. Fitted with a rising front, and rack and pinion focusing, it could take a first-class photograph, and its leather-covered body with black leather bellows and nickel- and black-enamel-finished metal parts would grace any collection.

The following list of the numbers of some of the early Kodak stereoscopic cameras sold outside the United States up to 1920 have been kindly made available by the Kodak Museum and will help collectors to

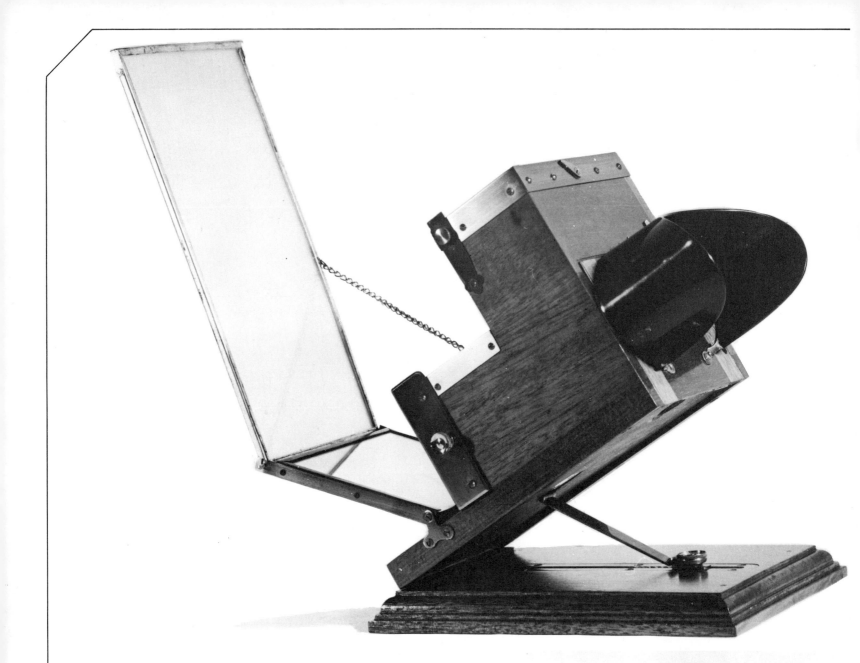

Ives Kromskop. The Kromscop photograph consist of three stereoscopic pairs of images each taken through a different coloured filter (red, green, and blue-violet). When combined in the Kromscop which had a similar set of filters, a coloured three dimensional image is produced.

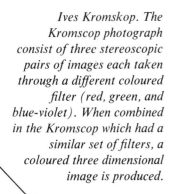

judge the comparative rarity of the different models. All these cameras were made in the United States, and it is estimated that three-quarters of the output was sold there. Where different, the names and model numbers by which they were known in Great Britain, is shown in brackets under the American name of each camera.

Camera	Date	Number sold in Great Britain	Numbers sold in Great Britain, Europe, India and South Africa
Stereo Weno No. 1	1901/1907	922	3,253
Stereo Weno No. 2 (Stereo Hawkeye No. 1)	1904/1907	125	480
No. 2 Stereo Kodak (Stereo Hawkeye No. 2)	1902/1908	504	997
No. 2 Stereo Brownie	1905/1911	503	1,725
Stereo Hawkeye No. 5 (No. 3)	1907/1919	184	643
Stereo Hawkeye No. 6 (No. 4)	1907/1919	406	1,242
Stereo Kodak Model I		61	220

(The figures for this camera are not complete as sales continued until 1925.)

By way of comparison, the figures for the early Kodak Panoramic cameras (from the same source) are also given here.

No. 1 Panoram Kodak	1900/1920	5,202	9,889
No. 4 Panoram Kodak	1900/1920	6,304	7,340

(The figures for both these Panoram Kodaks are not complete as sales continued until 1924.)

Collectors will see from these figures just how scarce these early stereoscopic cameras are and how necessary it is to preserve good examples of them.

These cameras illustrate an important phase in the history of photography, and even a few of them would be an asset to any camera collection. Putting together a complete set would be a most interesting and worthwhile project for any collector and is, in fact, one that I am working on myself.

At the turn of the century, many famous French firms were producing stereoscopic cameras that are now treasured by collectors. Mackenstein of Paris made several and one of the most interesting was the La Francia produced in 1900. It had a wooden body with a pair of $f\,4\cdot6$ lenses—which could be stopped down to $f\,192$!—and the rising front could also slide across, centring one of the lenses for panoramic photographs.

H. Bellieni Fils of Nancy in France also made an unusual wooden-bodied camera at this time. It was covered with brown leather measured $3'' \times 8\frac{1}{2}'' \times 7\frac{1}{2}''$, and had a pair of $f\,8$ lenses that could close down to $f\,156$ and focus from $1\cdot5$ m to infinity in a five-speed shutter on a rising front. Unconventionally, it took the two stereoscopic pictures on a

pair of individual $3'' \times 3\frac{1}{2}''$ (8×9 cm) plates.

Collectors will also revel in the wonderful range of stereoscopic cameras and viewers that were produced by Jules Richard of Paris, specialists in this field for some sixty years. Projectors for single frames, anaglyphic stereoscopic projectors, lanterns for viewing at night, automatic printers, attachments for binoculars, camera and outfit cases, slide boxes—the lists seem endless. To complete a collection of the Jules Richard stereoscopic cameras and accessories, from the earliest models to the Verascope F40 35mm camera which was undoubtedly the finest stereoscopic camera ever made and the last one that they produced, would almost be a work of a lifetime.

The Goerz Photo-Stereo-Binocular is an outstanding example of the many wonderful collectors' pieces that have come from Germany. Introduced in 1899, it was a combined $2\frac{1}{2} \times$ or $3\frac{1}{2} \times$ binocular and camera that could take either single or stereoscopic pairs of $1\frac{3}{4}'' \times 2\frac{1}{2}''$ plates. Another German camera was the Zeiss Stereo Palmas, made in 1908. It was one of the finest stereoscopic cameras of its day, and would make an exciting find for the collector. A complete outfit for it included a single lens panel, a normal stereoscopic twin lens panel, and a special stereoscopic lens panel for close-up photography.

Voigtländer produced several first-class stereoscopic cameras before World War I. For the collector the most interesting one was probably their Stereo-Panoram-Alpine camera. Taking $3\frac{1}{2}'' \times 5\frac{1}{2}''$ (10×15 cm) plates, it had a pair of $3\frac{1}{2}''$ (9 cm) and one $6''$ (15 cm) Collinear Series III lenses in a triple compound shutter. In 1907 however they introduced the Stereophotoscope. Made of metal, and with a changing box taking twelve of the now popular $1\frac{3}{4}'' \times 4\frac{1}{4}''$ (45×107 mm) plates, this was to be the forerunner of a long successful line of collectable stereoscopic cameras.

A new version of the Stereophotoscope produced in 1910 was fitted with a vertical rising front. A greatly improved model, the Stereoflectoscope, appeared in 1913 incorporating a central reflex viewfinder in place of the two viewfinders previously fitted. The focusing movement moved all three lenses simultaneously, allowing continuous viewing of a full-size picture.

The Cornu Ontoscope was one of the first-class stereoscopic cameras of this period, and one that will quicken the heart of any camera collector. Two sizes were available, 45 × 107 mm and 6 × 13 cm, and they were equipped with plate magazine, cut film magazines, single dark slides, and roll film backs, whilst a later 35 mm version taking a pair of 24 × 30 mm frames had a pair of 40 mm Berthiot f 3·5 lenses, and shutter speeds up to 1/100 second.

Many of these stereoscopic cameras from the early part of the twentieth century were made in very short runs, sometimes only twenty or thirty cameras in a batch. Owing to slight variations which occurred in the course of the manufacture of each order, and modifications which were often made at the customer's request, collectors will often find that parts of similar cameras are not interchangeable. This of course applies to many of the cameras made in those days, and the collector should keep a careful watch for the unusual models which are to be found even amongst the more common cameras.

Newman and Guardia produced outstanding cameras that are treasured by collectors today. Their stereoscopic roll film Special Sibyl is the most rare of all. It took 45 × 107 mm negatives on A116 (autographic) film and, according to one of their oldest employees who was a boy when these cameras were made in 1920, only one batch was turned out, probably not more than thirty in all.

The 'La Francia' wooden stereoscopic camera by Mackenstein of Paris used 78 × 180mm (3 1/10″ × 7 1/10″) plates 1900.

City Scale and Exchange of London sold this stereoscopic camera 1910. Courtesy of The Howarth-Loomes collection.

After World War I, Mr V.W. Edwards, who was in charge of the experimental department of Houghton's Limited of London, invented a small and novel stereoscopic camera taking two pairs of pictures on a single quarter-plate. Patented in 1921 this camera was never put into production, but a modified version taking twelve single 4·5 × 6 cm pictures on $2\frac{1}{4}$B roll film was introduced in 1922 as the Ensign-Cupid. The $3\frac{1}{4}″ × 3\frac{1}{4}″$ body of the Cupid was made of aluminium finished in black crystalline enamel, with black and nickel fittings. It had a direct vision viewfinder, time and instantaneous shutter (about 1/25 second), and an achromatic f 11 lens. I am indebted to Mr Edwards, who has allowed me to acquire this original prototype stereoscopic camera and the patent papers for my collection. Finding this sort of *rara avis* is a wonderful boost for a collector, and a collection which includes a camera that is 'the only one in the world' has an impact on all who see it.

LE **VÉRASCOPE**

ET LES **HOMÉOSCOPES**

Brevetés en tous pays

JULES RICHARD ❊, INGÉNIEUR-CONSTRUCTEUR

FONDATEUR ET SUCCESSEUR DE LA MAISON RICHARD FRÈRES

8, Impasse Fessart, PARIS-BELLEVILLE

TÉLÉPHONE N° 419-63

Adresse télégraphique :
ENREGISTREUR, PARIS

Homéoscope 8 × 9

Homéoscope 6 × 6 ¹/₂

Vérascope 4 ¹/₂ × 4 ¹/₂

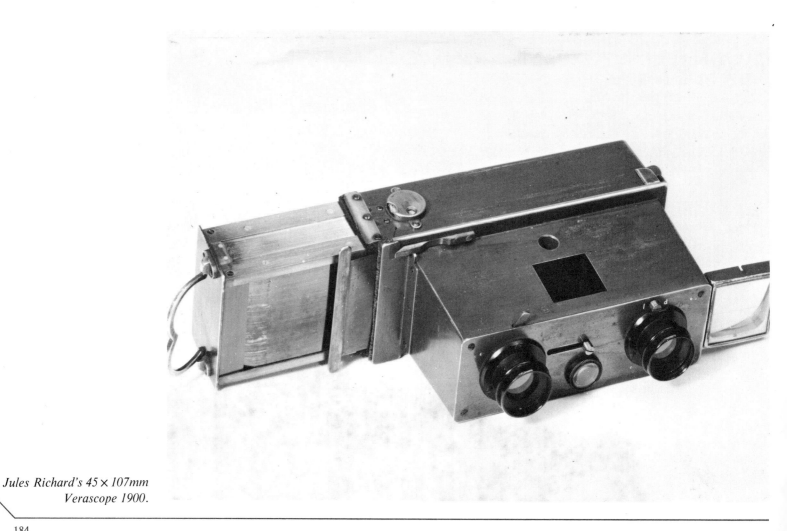

Another prototype that was never produced commercially was the Dopple-Leica. This was two Leicas assembled into one body for stereoscopic photography. Although the only prototype is in the Leica Museum at Wetzlar in Germany rumour has it that several others were in fact made, and 'escaped'. One of these would be a valuable find indeed.

Amongst English novelty stereoscopic cameras, the collector will find the Robin Hood made in 1930. This was a cheap plastic camera using cut film. The back was detachable, and was used as a developing dish and printing frame, and the camera was sold complete with a supply of film and printing paper, and chemicals for processing them. Although I paid only 50p for the one that I have, I was not really surprised when I saw one priced at £10 ($30) in a recent American catalogue of collector's cameras.

The Stereo Puck was another British stereo camera of the 1930s, and is one that can be found more easily by collectors. It was a box camera which took eight pairs of pictures on 120 roll film. Three versions of it were made by the Thornton-Pickard Manufacturing Company. No. 1 was the standard model, No. 2 had built-in close-up lenses for portraits, and No. 3 was a special model that had a slide for covering one of the lenses so that it could be used for taking single photographs in addition to the stereo pairs.

The K.B. Lentic camera, with its six lenses for producing lenticular stereoscopic prints, would be a unique find. Unfortunately when I finally managed to locate one of these for my collection and chased after it, I arrived too late. It had been dismantled, the lenses sold, and the body scrapped. Very few of these cameras were made, and they are very hard to find indeed.

A small representative collection of the many devices that have been produced to make stereoscopic pairs of pictures with single lens cameras would be an interesting offshoot to a collection of stereoscopic cameras. Apparatus designed for making stereoscopic pairs with a single exposure of an ordinary single lens camera can also be collected. Simple beam-splitters using mirrors, better models using prisms, and still more sophisticated ones which turn the pairs of images on to their sides so as to create a wide screen horizontal format rather than the vertical pictures produced by ordinary beam-splitters, have all been marketed from time to time.

The collecting of stereograms has a fascination all of its own. Examples can be found covering the entire field of photography from the earliest daguerreotypes right up to the stereograms of the moon's surface that were taken by the first men on the moon.

Stereoscopic pairs of pictures were produced by all the early photographic processes, but the earliest collectable examples to be found today are stereoscopic daguerreotypes. Whether this is due to the permanency of the silver-coated copper plates used, compared with the frailty of the paper of the early calotype prints, or because of the popularity of the daguerreotype itself, it is difficult to judge. It was however the introduction of wet collodion plates in 1950 that led to the really large-scale production of stereograms.

A. Ferrier in France, the Langenheim Brothers in Philadelphia, and E. Anthony in New York, were notable early pioneers who led the flood of photographers in this field. The Langenheims used the albumen on glass process for producing stereograms in the early 1850s, and Ferrier is credited with making them in 1851. These slides can still be found, and should be treasured and carefully preserved. An 1854 glass stereogram

Brass reinforced wooden tropical cameras are highly thought of by collectors and stereoscopic ones are extremely rare. This beautiful example made of mahogany with red leather trim is the tropical stereoscopic version of the Soho reflex camera made by Marion and Co. 1921.

Thornton-Pickard 'Puck' stereoscopic 120 roll film box camera 1934.

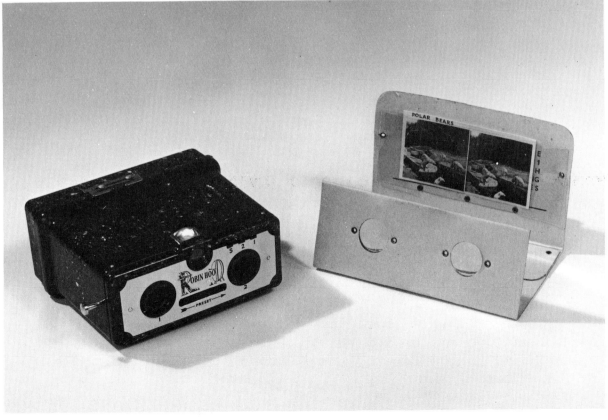

Standard Cameras 'Robin Hood' stereoscopic camera was an inexpensive bakelite camera that was sold complete with sheet film, gaslight paper, chemical and a folding viewer, 1930.

*Newman and Guardias'
stereoscopic roll film
Special Sibyl is the most rare
of all their cameras, 1920.*

*The Russian Sputnik was
probably the last stereoscopic
camera to produce pairs of
$2\frac{1}{4}'' \times 2\frac{1}{4}''$ frames. Made of
plastic it was imported into
Britain by Duval Ltd. who
sold it as the Duval
stereoscopic camera, 1956.*

of Genesee Falls was listed by Tom and Elinor Burnside in their catalogue *Daguerian Era* for winter 1972/3 at £30 ($75). This seems to be a very high price for a single glass slide but, as they say, it is extremely rare.

Glass stereograms were made in Britain and Europe from the early 1850s until World War I. Albumen plates were used at first and, as the new processes came into use, collodion wet plates (between 1860 and 1880), and then dry plates, were employed. Great rarities amongst the early stereograms are prints on tissue paper bound in glass plates, and those on porcelain, and ferrotype plates (tinplates).

From the middle 1850s most commercial stereograms were prints mounted on $3\frac{1}{2}'' \times 7''$ cards, though some $\frac{1}{2}''$ higher measuring $4'' \times 7''$ were made during the 1870s and 1880s. Until the early 1860s the Langenheims often used the same negatives to make stereograms on both glass and card mounts.

In Britain, George Swan Nottage started the London Stereoscopic Company in 1854 and from a very small beginning, making stereoscopes, it grew so rapidly that by 1856 he had sold over half a million stereoscopes and millions of stereograms for them. This gives some indication of the craze for stereoscopes and stereograms that swept the whole of the civilized world at that time, and will help collectors to realize the vast scope that exists for collecting them.

Many stereograms were hand coloured. These were first introduced in Britain in 1853, and they were first made in America by the Langenheims in 1854. They were manufactured for about twenty years and during that time large numbers of stereograms were made both in the usual black, or sepia and white, and in hand-coloured versions. The better examples were usually those made in Britain, many of which are really beautifully coloured. But lovely ones were also made in the United States and France. Pairs of the same stereogram, one plain and the other coloured, make interesting exhibits in a collection.

The earliest card stereograms had square corners until the late 1860s, when the corners began to be rounded off. This lessened the wear and tear on the cards, as it was found that the corners were often damaged in use, and it will help the collector to date his early cards.

A French invention of 1864, which is well worth looking for, is the tissue stereogram. In this, the photographs were printed on semi-transparent tissue paper, framed in cardboard, and backed with a second piece of plain tissue which was usually hand coloured. From about 1868 many of these tissues were made with small pinholes pricked or cut out for lights, jewellery, eyes, doors and windows etc. Illuminated from the rear, these brought further life to the transparencies.

Favourite subjects for these tissues were *diable* scenes (table-top photographs of skeletons and devils in 'Gruesome Scenes in Hell') and ballet scenes, but many different views can also be found.

These tissues were mainly made in France, and only for a period of about ten years between 1864 and 1874. A small number were manufactured in other European countries and in Britain, and a very small number were made in America around 1900. These American tissues are very rare indeed.

When stereoscopes are bought by collectors, they are often accompanied by a bundle of stereograms, and many collections have been started in this way. The cataloguing of stereograms should be started as soon as the first ones are acquired, otherwise the collector will soon be faced with boxes of unsorted and unlisted slides, and the

collection will suffer accordingly.

Many collectors specialize in stereograms of one subject or type. Others collect stereograms that supplement their other interests. American 'Wild West' fans look for stereograms of Indian chiefs, famous cowboys, and associated views, while railway enthusiasts collect stereograms showing early engines and rolling stock, as well as those showing the building of new lines, and scenes of the countryside along the way.

French 'Diable'
tissue stereogram 1868.

At Bilbao Railway Station,
stereogram 1863.

The stereograms with the greatest interest to camera collectors are those showing photographers at work with their apparatus and accessories and most of us keep a sharp look out for these. They are not often come across but a card stereogram of Niagara Falls was recently sold for £1 ($2.50) at a public auction, mainly because only one of the collectors present noticed the photographer and his camera at work in a corner of the slide. A more realistic price for an

*Archery Ground,
Bournemouth,
stereogram 1863.*

*Free Niagara Prospect
Point winter,
stereogram 1895.*

image of this nature was the £70 that was paid at Sotheby's on the 1st August 1972 for a sixth-plate ambrotype showing a frock-coated photographer three-quarter length with his wet-plate camera and tripod.

Stereograms of wars from the earliest days of photography are also highly valued by collectors. During the American Civil

Teahouse in China stereogram by George Rose of Melbourne, Australia 1890.

War photographers followed both the Union and Confederate armies, many of them taking the popular stereoscopic pictures. Perhaps the most well known are those that were taken by the team of photographers organized by Mathew Brady. Photographs and stereograms taken by these men are as eagerly sought after by collectors as those taken by Brady himself.

*Selection of stereoscopic
cigarette cards:–*

*Very rare Australian card
with two small photographs
of 'Ascot Sunday'.*

*Two standard size cards
'Tyrannosaurus Rex' from*
Peeps into Prehistoric
Times *1930*

*Two large size cards 'Niagara
Falls' from the second series
of* Peeps into Many
Lands *1928.*

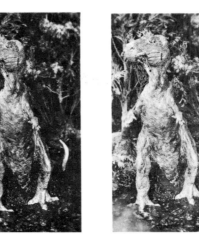

NIAGARA FALLS. AMERICA.

The stereograms of the Franco-Prussian War of 1870–71 were the last to be made using the wet-plate process. The Spanish-American War of 1898, the Boer War of 1899–1902, and the Russo-Japanese War of 1904–5, were all covered by photographers using dry plate or film cameras, and large sets of stereograms were issued by many firms. Between wars, events everywhere were covered by stereo photographs, bringing the wonders of the world into the parlours of the people. Exhibitions and inventions, disasters, the crowning of kings and the inaugurations of presidents, the gold rush in Alaska and life in Australia – stereograms were made of them all, and a vast variety can still be found and collected. With the large numbers still available the collector should discard seriously damaged or defaced stereograms and concentrate on building up a collection of slides in the best possible condition.

Collecting – and using – stereoscopic cameras and equipment is a very satisfying and rewarding hobby, but fellow photographers will sympathise with the correspondent who, in reply to one of my letters enquiring after early stereoscopic cameras, wrote: 'Sorry, but I have nothing in the way of stereo gear; I have enough trouble taking one picture at a time, let alone two!'

INDEX OF CAMERAS

INDEX

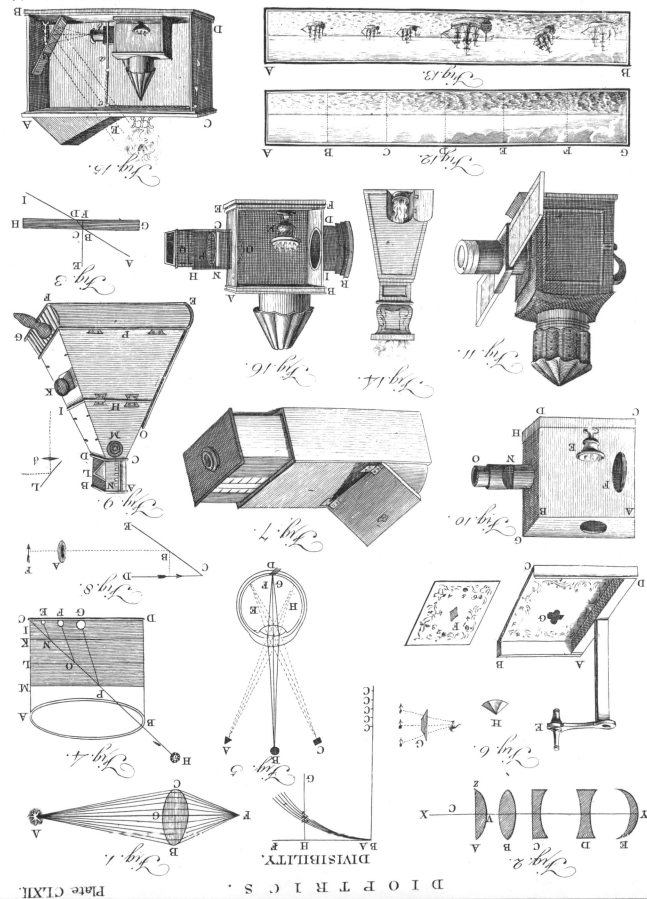

Plate CLXII.   D I O P T R I C S .